D0426785

THE STUDY OF
OLD TESTAMENT
THEOLOGY TODAY

by

EDWARD J. YOUNG

FLEMING H. REVELL COMPANY

Westwood, New Jersey
London E.C.4—29 Ludgate Hill
Glasgow C.2—229 Bothwell Street

Library of Congress Catalog Card Number: 59-10094

Printed in the United States of America

1.1

PREFACE

THE present volume contains four lectures which were delivered at the London Bible College, London, England, at the dedication of its new building in May, 1958. This college stands true to the infallible Scriptures and is carrying on a valiant work in the training of Christian workers who will conduct a genuine Biblical ministry.

In discussing Old Testament theology, my purpose was not so much to consider the various efforts which are today being made to carry out the study as to pay attention to certain factors which must be taken into consideration in any proper treatment of the subject. This has led me, however, to contrast these efforts with a proper Biblical approach.

The Bible is a revelation from God, and when we consider the historical revelations which God made to His people, we are studying Old Testament Biblical theology. In other words, Old Testament theology, if we are to be guided by the Bible in our definition, is nothing more nor less than the study of God in His self-revelation in the history of redemption.

There remains the pleasant task of expressing my gratitude to the faculty and students of the London Bible College for the many kindnesses which they showed me. I am particularly grateful to Principal Ernest F. Kevan, and would take this opportunity to express my admiration for the work that he is doing. In the preparation of a book there is the typing of a manuscript, and those who perform this arduous task often receive little recognition. I am ever grateful to Mrs. Richard Marsh for the careful manner in which she prepared the typescript.

EDWARD J. YOUNG

CONTENTS

Lecture I

OLD TESTAMENT THEOLOGY
AND HISTORY

ONE who examines carefully the present theological climate of opinion cannot but be struck by the rapidity with which it has supplanted and is supplanting theological positions of a former day. The change has been rapid, indeed, so rapid, that some, it would seem, have not yet been able to catch their theological breath. At one moment we found ourselves in an atmosphere which exalted man and his powers and at the same time depreciated and disparaged doctrine. Today such an attitude seems strange. On all hands we hear of the importance of doctrine and of theology. We are told that we must not place too great an emphasis upon human ability, but must rather stress the grace of God. And we must be biblical, passionately biblical, in all our thinking.

(a) The Present Interest in Old Testament Theology

Towards the close of the last century, it may be said that there existed a certain climate of theological opinion. That climate was the result of long years of growth. Undergirding the entire picture and foundational to it was the Darwinian theory of evolution with its consequent belief in the inevitable progress and advance of mankind toward the higher and the better.[1] In the field of New Testament studies the purely human Jesus of Adolph Harnack was on the throne.[2] And in the realm of the Old Testament the reconstruction of Israel's history and religion as it had been popularly presented by Wellhausen,

7

was in a position of dominance. As has often been noted, Wellhausen's reconstruction was somewhat influenced by the philosophical views of Hegel, and these views were congenial to the general tenor of thought of the day.[3] When we turn to the field of theology, we note that the position of Albrecht Ritschl with his emphasis upon value judgments was influential.[4] All of those views and tendencies seemed to be complementary. All fitted in quite comfortably with the prevailing stress upon the inherent goodness of man. Furthermore, all of them could be and were popularized. They expressed themselves in the churches as that phenomenon which, for want of a better term, is commonly designated "modernism". Man was told, in effect, how good he was, and how unimportant doctrine was. Not creed, but life, was the slogan, for doctrine divides, but service unites. The words of Pope were, in effect, made the slogan of the entire world of thought of the time:

> For modes of faith let graceless zealots fight.
> He can't be wrong whose life is in the right.[5]

Modernism, however, never asked, at least in any serious manner, by what standard one could judge whether a person's life was in the right. Today, modernism, in its older form, appears to be on the wane. The heart has been taken out of it. This is not to say that it does not linger on here and there, but the "older" modernism, with the force that it presented in the decade 1920–30, is no longer present.

Today, an entirely different climate of opinion is about us. It is the fashion at present in some circles to decry evolution, and to place great stress and emphasis upon the importance and significance of doctrine. Theology once again is being regarded as the queen of the sciences. Undergirding both New and Old Testament studies is that method of approach commonly known as Form

Criticism.[6] In the Old Testament field many of the positions once espoused by Wellhausen have been rejected. For the most part that aspect of his views which may be called the Development Hypothesis has been discarded, while most scholars today do agree with him in advocating some form of Documentary Hypothesis.[7] Undergirding much of modern thought is the philosophy of Immanuel Kant, and, in the field of theology, dialecticism and existentialism wield a tremendous influence.

Whereas the older complex of views paid little attention thereto, the dominant complex has much to say about theology. Inasmuch as we are concerned primarily with Old Testament theology, we shall seek to note, in particular, what it has to say—and it has much to say—about the subject. In the field of Old Testament studies theology has become quite popular, and books on the subject are appearing with some frequency.

According to Von Rad, who has published an extremely interesting work on the subject, Old Testament theology is one of the most recent of all the Biblical sciences.[8] Its history, he says, dates from the end of the eighteenth and the beginning of the nineteenth centuries, and that history can be told rapidly. It is worthy of note, he continues, that up until today it has not been possible to reach agreement as to the object of the science. The research of the last twenty to thirty years (Von Rad wrote in May, 1957) has helped in this respect, however, for it has brought about a surprising *rapprochement* between the science of Introduction and Biblical Theology.[9]

In the sense in which Von Rad employs the term, Old Testament theology is a comparatively late science. The first representative of the subject is usually thought to be Gabler.[10] Many of the older commentaries also contain material on the subject. One who works through the writings of the old masters, such as Hengstenberg, Keil,

Drechsler, or Delitzsch, will find that there is much in their writings that can truly be designated Old Testament theology. The same, however, is true of the writings of the reformers, Calvin and Luther, and for that matter, of some of the fathers. But the study of Old Testament theology as a science probably takes its rise with the work of Gabler. We may also note, in passing, the emphasis that was recently given to this subject by the late Geerhardus Vos at a time when the climate of opinion spoke more favourably of Histories of the Religion of Israel than of Old Testament Theology.

(b) The Background of the Present Interest

What are the causes which have led to the present revival of emphasis upon the subject? Perhaps this question cannot be fully answered. It is probable, however, and this is acknowledged by some who do not accept the full trustworthiness of Scripture, that the barrenness of the negative critical study of the Old Testament during the nineteenth century led to a reaction. During this century there was much emphasis upon the analysis of documents, and upon the so-called minutiae of "criticism". Was the Old Testament, however, merely a book to dissect into documents? When one had determined the extent of J, E, D and P and of any minor documents, had he done his full task? More and more, the same type of scholar who, had he been living in the nineteenth century, would, as far as one can tell, have fallen in line with the then dominant approach to the Old Testament, is now crying out that there is after all something more to the Bible than mere documentary analysis. The Bible, it is being said, has an abiding message; it speaks to the men of our day, and our task is to discover what that message is.

If this nineteenth-century study of the Old Testament in fact was so barren, one may wonder why the discovery was not made sooner. Those who engaged in the study itself apparently did not think that it was barren, and they were strong in their opposition to the view that the Bible was a special revelation from God. There must then have been another and deeper reason for the shift from the practice of mere documentary analysis to that of study of the content of the Old Testament. For our part we think that this shift was brought about by factors such as the discoveries of archaeology and the tragic events in the world during recent years. Archaeology has shown that the Old Testament history is far more trustworthy than was acknowledged by Wellhausen and others of his day, and it has in general supported the position of those who regard the Bible as trustworthy.

The two tragic wars which our century has witnessed have caused men to ask the question whether man himself is, as a matter of fact, inherently good. Earlier thinkers and writers had, in effect, challenged the easygoing assumption that man was not a fallen and depraved creature. Kierkegaard, although he did not write from the standpoint of Biblical orthodoxy, has had a deep influence, and Dostoevski in his novels has portrayed mankind as depraved. One cannot read *Crime and Punishment* and at the same time speak of the inherent goodness of human nature. Nor does the vicious cruelty which the recent wars exhibited speak well of mankind. A shift in theological emphasis was bound to come.

What shall we say about this shift in emphasis? Is it a return to the orthodoxy of the Church, to the true teaching of Holy Scripture? Is it a re-emphasis upon that wondrous saving Gospel of salvation which has brought life and hope to so many thousands who were in the bondage of sin? Apparently there are some who think that this is so. If, on the other hand, it is not entirely to be identified with the historic position of the Church, is it, at least, a step in that direction? Is it, in effect, a return to the Reformation?

These questions, we think, can be answered fairly easily. Whatever else the modern emphasis may be, it is not a revival of orthodoxy. Its advocates are the last people in the world who would want to be known as orthodox, and to seek to identify this revival of theology with orthodox Christianity is to mistake its true character.

The modern emphasis upon Old Testament theology fits in well with modern thought. It is perfectly willing, to mention but one aspect of the question, to make use of a criticism of the Bible which leads to results contrary to the Bible's own testimony. This may be seen, for example, by Von Rad's approach to the study of the traditions of Israel. Von Rad aligns himself at once on the side of what is today called the traditio-historical method of investigation, and takes issue with the older literary criticism.[11] This older literary criticism, he says, believed that standing more or less immediately behind the present literary form of the books there was the historical course of events, at least, in their essentials, and that literary criticism could grasp this course of events. We now know, however, he says, that such is not so. At best, we can simply find definite conceptions and representations of old traditions which go back to different circles. In studying each unit of tradition we must apply the method of Form Criticism. The individual narrative units which we find in the documents J and E have a long history behind them. At first, says Von Rad, they stood alone, independent, but in course of time they came to be incorporated in the great blocks of tradition, and these blocks of tradition were themselves later joined together in accordance with a definite theological picture of sacred history (*Heilsgeschichte*)[12].

It is difficult for us today, so the argument continues, to

obtain knowledge of the historical events in this early period because the framework of the Hexateuchal tradition has been destroyed and a cultic-canonical scheme has predominated. Another factor which makes the early history of Israel difficult to study is the fact that the present sources support the tradition that the nation arose in Egypt. But historical investigation has shown that the word "Israel" was used only as the designation of the sacral tribal bond, which was constituted only after the entrance of the individual tribes into Canaan.[13]

It should be apparent that Von Rad employs a method of approach which is perfectly willing to make use of a "criticism" that will lead to results which conflict with the Bible's witness to itself. We have mentioned Von Rad's work because it is one of the latest and most competent treatises upon the subject of Old Testament theology. And whereas not all writers are willing to accept a position so radical as that of Von Rad, he may nevertheless be justly singled out as a most capable representative of one aspect of the modern emphasis upon Old Testament theology.

(c) The Historical Setting of Old Testament Theology

We may perhaps arrive at a better evaluation of modern Old Testament theology, and at a better understanding of Old Testament theology in general, if we study it in relation to history. The religion of the Bible is a religion that is founded squarely upon certain things that God did in history. According to the Bible, there was a very definite intrusion of the supernatural into the affairs of men. As the late J. Gresham Machen put it, "The centre and core of all the Bible is history. Everything else that the Bible contains is fitted into an historical framework and leads up to an historical climax. The Bible is primarily a record of events."[14] It is in this manner that the great saving events of Old Testament history are presented. "I am the

LORD thy God, which brought thee out of the land of Egypt, out of the house of bondage". (Exodus xx, 2)

The teaching of this text is perfectly clear. God is here represented as speaking to the nation as a unit. He speaks to the entire nation, it should be noted, and not to a few individual tribes. According to this work of the Lord, the nation as a unit was once in the land of Egypt, which to it was a house of bondage. There was a time when the nation of Israel was in bondage to the nation of Egypt. Such a condition did not continue, however, for Israel was relieved of her bondage, in that God Himself brought her out of Egypt. God intervened in human history and wrought the deliverance which set Israel free.

It must ever be remembered that everything which occurs takes place because God has so decreed it. We may see the hand of God in all things that take place round about us, and in all the events of history. There is also a certain sense in which we may legitimately speak of God's working in any event of history. It is God's providential working. Is this providential working of God in history that to which this particular verse of Exodus has reference? The answer is no. This verse clearly teaches that the Exodus from Egypt was the result of a special work of God. It follows that any description of the Exodus as an historical event, if one would do justice to this particular verse, must include the statement that God Himself brought Israel out of Egypt. God, according to this verse, did intervene in the history of Israel in a special way.

We may note another example, namely, the account of the Fall, which is recorded in the third chapter of Genesis. Whatever we today may think about the course of events there depicted, it would seem that the writer of this chapter believed that he was writing an account of something that in fact took place on this earth. It would seem that he believed that there was such a place as the

Garden of Eden, else why his detailed attempt to locate the Garden? He believed that there was a man named Adam and a woman named Eve, and that a serpent spoke to them. By an act of disobedience upon the part of Adam, according to the author of Genesis, sin entered the world. The account does not bear the marks of legend or parable. Nor is there the slightest evidence to support the position that the writer thought he was recounting the experience of every man. The writer in no way indicates that he thought he was writing about his own experience.

We today may say that we do not believe that the events recorded in the third chapter of Genesis took place, but we do not have warrant for the assumption that the writer himself did not think that he was penning history. The man who says, "The writer of the third chapter of Genesis thought that he was writing history but I do not believe that history" is a better exegete than the man who says that the events recorded in the third chapter of Genesis are profoundly true but that the writer never intended them to be taken as history.

The religion presented in the Old Testament, then, according to its own representation, is an historical religion. It is grounded upon that which God Himself did in history. Remove this historical foundation from it and there is no longer any true biblical religion. There can be no true Old Testament theology, unless it does justice to the historical basis upon which it must rest. To be truly biblical, Old Testament theology must pay due heed to the requirements of history.

At this point we must give consideration to a word that has featured prominently in recent discussions of Old Testament theology. It is the word *Heilsgeschichte*. This word *Heilsgeschichte* simply means "history of salvation" or "salvation history" or "holy history". In itself, it would seem to represent a thoroughly Biblical concept, namely, the fact that God through the ages has carried out His purpose of redeeming mankind. There is surely a certain sense in which all things subserve this purpose of God in redemption. "All things", the inspired writer says, "work together for good to them that love God, to them who are the called according to his purpose." (Romans viii, 28) It is consequently to be expected that students of Scripture would trace and would emphasize the great saving events of biblical history. We may expect Christian students to devote more time to the Exodus from Egypt, for example, than to what the book of Exodus has to say about the Amalekites. This does not mean for a moment that what the Exodus has to say about the Amalekites is unimportant. It is important, for it provides a part of the background against which the redeeming acts of God are the better to be understood. Important as it is, however, what the Bible has to say about the Amalekites is certainly not so immediately relevant to us and to our needs, as is that which it has to say about the Exodus itself.

It is understandable, therefore, that scholars should devote more attention to the primary message of Scripture, namely, God's gracious saving work. One need but examine the writings of the commentators who lived before Reformation times to discover that this is so. It was also true of Luther and Calvin, although neither of these dismissed any portion of Scripture as of no consequence. This fact must be stressed, despite the emphasis which today is placed upon Luther's words that that is Scripture which presents Christ (*was Christum treibet*).

In post-Reformation times we may note the work of George Calixtus, *De pactis quae Deus cum hominibus iniit* (1656) in which the author sought to show how God had made various covenants with man and that in these covenants there was a progressive revelation. In this work doctrine was not divorced from history, but rather history was made its setting and background. God worked in human history, and in this history He established His covenant with man.

At a much later time, J. C. K. von Hofmann also stressed the history of redemption, laying emphasis upon the importance of Messianic prophecy.[15] The full significance of a particular prophecy was not discernible at the time of its utterance, he maintained, but only in the light of the history of redemption itself, which would find its completion in the end of the ages. With this work of von Hofmann in mind, we may well ask the question, "What can be said about *Heilsgeschichte* in present-day study of the Old Testament?"

At this stage it is necessary to make an important distinction. The Germans have two words which may be translated by the English word history, namely, *Historie* and *Geschichte*. As the word *Historie* is employed, it seems to be the equivalent of what we normally speak of as history. An event which occurs in *Historie* is an historical event. It took place on this earth and on a definite day of the calendar. Napoleon was defeated at Waterloo on 18 June, 1815. That is an historical event. It belongs to *Historie*. It occurred at a certain place and on a certain calendar day. It may be the object of investigation upon the part of the historian. Historians may differ in their interpretation of the event and of the reasons which brought it to pass. They may not be able, for one reason or another, to learn all that there is to learn about the event, but that it was an event which took place here upon this earth at a particular place and on a particular day is a fact which, unless all the sources are deliberately deceiving us, has occurred.

What, however, is to be said about the word *Geschichte*? This word also means "history", and sometimes is employed as a synonym for *Historie*. We may legitimately speak, for example, of a *Geschichte des deutschen Volkes*, and when we find a volume with such a title, we have every warrant for believing that it will be an account of the history of the German people. We may also employ the word in speaking of the history of Israel. And the word may certainly be legitimately used in speaking of the history of redemption.

Is there not, however, another sense in which the word is often employed today? Does not Karl Barth, to take but one example, use the word in quite a different sense? It is at this stage that the modern approach to Christianity makes itself apparent. The word *Geschichte* is often employed today, not in the sense of history, as that word is commonly understood, but rather to designate some other realm, such as that which is above history. By way of example, we may cite the Resurrection of Jesus Christ. According to the Bible and the traditional belief of the Church, the body of Jesus Christ came to life on the third day by means of a mighty miracle. The Resurrection is thus seen to be an historical event. There was a tomb at a particular spot in Palestine, and in this tomb the dead body of the Lord was placed. On the third day, a particular calendar day of our history, that tomb was empty, and the reason why it was empty was that God performed a miracle. The body of the Lord emerged from the tomb. Christ rose from the dead. Paul puts it with singular force, "And if Christ be not risen, then is our preaching vain, and your faith is also vain. Yea, and we are found false witnesses of God; because we have testified of God that he raised up Christ: whom he raised not up, if so be that the dead rise not. For if the dead rise not, then is not Christ raised: And if Christ be not raised, your faith is vain; ye are yet in your sins." (1 Corinthians xv, 14–17) If there is anything clear in the Bible, it is that the Lord Jesus Christ rose from the dead. The resurrection, according to the Bible, is an historical event.

Today, however, the word *Geschichte* is often applied to the resurrection. The resurrection is true, it is said, but it belongs to the realm of *Geschichte*. Thus, Barth himself, thinks that the resurrection should not necessarily be thought of as following chronologically the death of Christ.[16] It is not, therefore, to be understood as an historical event, in the sense in which that term has been hitherto employed.

When we turn to the Old Testament we may note the account of the Fall. This account, it is said sometimes, belongs to the realm of *Heilsgeschichte*. What, then, is the precise connotation that we are to put upon the word in this instance? Paul, in Romans v, evidently regarded the Fall as an historical event when he contrasted it with the work of Christ. And it has been well said that if Paul did not consider the work of Adam to be historical, then consistency would lead us to conclude that he also did not consider the work of Christ to be historical. But was Paul correct in his interpretation of the Fall? Was the Fall an historical event?

To ask this question is to answer it. With respect to the Fall, we are often told, we can no longer hold to the old orthodox view of a literal fall into sin. The account, however, is to be interpreted in various ways. It is said to be a parable, a type, or to belong to the spiritual realm. Other words are also employed. It is said to be *Urgeschichte*, it is supra-temporal or supra-historical; it belongs to the realm of faith or to the realm of redemption, or the realm where scientific research is to no avail. Whatever be the precise connotation of these and kindred terms, it is perfectly clear that some advocates of what today is called *Heilsgeschichte* do not regard the Fall as an historical event. In this attitude toward the Fall they are thus at variance with the Apostle Paul and also, it may be noted, with Jesus Christ Himself.

With respect to the account of the Fall, it would seem that some are willing to regard it as part of th content of *Heilsgeschichte*, and yet to deny its true historical character. This raises the question, Are the great saving events of God which are today designated as constituting *Heilsgeschichte* in fact historical events or are they not? It is our opinion that if this question were given a forthright answer, that answer would have to be no. In reality, the question is often evaded, and no clear-cut reply is given to it. But it calls for, indeed it demands, an answer, and we have every right to insist upon an answer being given.

The approach to the subject, however, which is made today, is one which often avoids a direct answer. We do not say that there is a deliberate attempt made to evade the question, but there surely is a lack of facing up to the question and what it involves. Thus Von Rad, to take one of the most competent writers, tells us that the subject for investigation on the part of the Old Testament theologian is what Israel herself said about God. Israel knew that she was a nation founded on historical facts and beheld herself formed and moulded by facts in which she saw the hand of God active. That, says Von Rad, is the object of study for Old Testament theological science.

The matter has also been brilliantly set forth in a little book by Professor G. Ernest Wright, *God Who Acts*. The key thought is to be found in the sub-title, *Biblical Theology as Recital*.[17] It might be called Theology by Inference. This work of Wright is one of the clearest statements of one aspect of the modern position, and deserves careful study. The heart of the whole matter is stated in the preface, where it is said that biblical theology " . . . is a theology of recital or proclamation of the acts of God, together with the inferences drawn therefrom".[18] We have been accustomed to speak of the Bible as the "Word of God". It would be better, however, to speak of it as the

"Acts of God". "Biblical theology", Wright claims, "is the confessional recital of the redemptive acts of God in a particular history, because history is the chief medium of revelation."[19]

Perhaps the key to what Wright is saying is found in the thought that the knowledge of God had been inferred from what had in fact happened in human history. The force of this statement will become apparent if we consider one of the great "acts of God" to which special attention is today being devoted, namely, the Exodus from Egyptian bondage. We are told that in the events connected with the Exodus the Israelites saw the hand of God. From these acts they inferred that God was present, and that it was their own God, Yahweh, who was bringing them out of the house of bondage. They had been slaves in a particularly cruel period of bondage. Now, however, the yoke of the oppressor was to be overthrown, and they were to be delivered from Egypt. They were able to leave the land and to find freedom for themselves in the Sinai Peninsula. What, however, was the cause of their deliverance? How had it come about that they were set free? Was it not their own God, Yahweh, the God whom Moses had met at the burning bush, who had delivered them? Were not the wondrous things which they saw accomplished in fact works of God Himself? It was this conclusion to which the Israelites came. God Himself—their God, Yahweh—was working for them. They saw His hand in action, and they believed that He had delivered them from Egypt.

Before we make an analysis of this interpretation we should note that other peoples also have believed that their gods were active in the events of their lives. Hattusilis, for example, the great Hittite king, was fully confident that he had been placed on the throne by the goddess Ishtar. He praises Ishtar for what she has done. On this point he was very explicit. "I tell the divine power of Ishtar," he said, "may men hear it."[20] Among his descendants he desired that there should be reverence for Ishtar. Ishtar had "chosen" Hattusilis; she had desired him to be her priest. "In the hand of Ishtar, my lady, I saw prosperity," he claims.[21] The favour of Ishtar aroused enmity on the part of others, but Ishtar rescued him.[22] In fact, because of her protection, others could not prevail against him. In battle he was victorious, for Ishtar marched before him.[23] In family life, for the same reason, he was happy.[24] Finally, because of Ishtar, Hattusilis was placed upon the throne.[25] "And Ishtar my lady," he says, "gave me also the kingship of the land of Hatti and I became a great king." Throughout the account, the king speaks as one who is confident that the goddess Ishtar is with him.[26] Let us concentrate upon the claims of Hattusilis. This king believed that Ishtar, the goddess, had wrought wondrous things for him. In the events of his life he inferred that Ishtar was working. Wherein lay the difference between the inferences of Hattusilis and those of Israel? There were many differences. The Israelites believed that God had truly been responsible for, in fact had been active in, their deliverance. On the one hand, we have a nation, or at least, a few tribes, whereas, on the other, we simply have an individual. Furthermore, the faith of Israel grew into something, whereas that of Hattusilis did not. When all this has been said, however, we have not yet reached the heart of the matter. How shall we analyse the inferences which Hattusilis made? Shall we regard them as mere religious talk, such as was common to the kings of antiquity? Shall we look upon them as expressing a kind of superstition? Did the king in fact think that the goddess, Ishtar, had brought victory to him and had placed him on the throne? Perhaps we cannot answer these questions. We do not know very much about the man Hattusilis as an individual. But then, we do not know very much about the Israelites as individuals. And if some modern theories are correct, we do not even know the identity of the Israelites who composed the account of the Exodus. We know more about Hattusilis as an individual, it would seem, than we do about the authors of the Exodus account. How, then, can we possibly tell why they made these inferences? The answer that is given is that they made these inferences because they truly believed that God was at work in the events of the Exodus.

Whatever may have led Hattusilis to make the inferences that he did (if we may legitimately speak of his having made inferences), we may be sure that he was mistaken. He may have inferred that Ishtar had placed him on the throne. In fact, however, we know that Ishtar did not place him on the throne. Ishtar had nothing whatever to do with Hattusilis, and the reason why we know this for a fact is that there is not, nor was there ever, any Ishtar. Hattusilis, therefore, was an adherent of a false religion. He believed, if his words are to be taken with any seriousness at all, in the existence of a goddess who did not exist. His inference from the events in which he was involved, if inference it was, was wholly mistaken, and not worthy of serious consideration.

What, however, shall we say about the inferences which Israel supposedly made from the events of the Exodus? Israel thought that she saw in these events the hand of her God, Yahweh. The all-important question is this, Was Israel's inference true to fact or was it not? That is the question that must be answered if there is to be a true and a proper understanding of the events of the Exodus. How is this question to be answered? For that matter, upon what basis may we answer the question whether Ishtar existed or not? Israel inferred that her God, Yahweh, was at work in delivering her from the bondage of Egypt in which she had found herself. Was Yahweh, however, as a matter of fact, so at work? Was Israel drawing a true inference from what she experienced, or was she simply deceived? These questions are important. If Israel, like Hattusilis, was mistaken in her inference, then it is of little importance whether we study the theology of the Old Testament or not. If the ancient writers of the Old Testament thought that Yahweh had brought them out of Egypt, whereas, in fact, Yahweh had not brought them out of Egypt, their inferences were false, and are of no more relevance or importance than are the inferences which the ancient Greeks, for example, made about the workings of the gods in their lives.

(d) The Necessity for Christian-Theistic Presuppositions

How are we to arrive at a proper answer to these questions? How can we today tell whether Israel was true to fact in her inferences? If we are to study Old Testament theology as it should be studied, we must first notice that true Old Testament theology rests upon a Christian-theistic position. Apart from Christian theism, Old Testament theology can have no validity; indeed, there can then be no real Old Testament theology. Christian theism presupposes the existence of the one ever-living and true God, the Creator of heaven and earth. It presupposes that He is the source of all wisdom and knowledge. All areas of human life derive their meaning from Him. In His light we see light. Wisdom and power are His, and they are derived from Him. He is not a part of the world process, nor is He dependent upon the world. Rather, He is the Creator, who by the will of His power has brought all things into existence. All things, apart from Him, owe their origin and being to Him. All are dependent on Him, but He is not dependent on them. He exists independently of them, for, in the truest sense of the word, He is the

Creator. He is One who is distinct from us, to whom we can say "Thou". He is one whom we can love, and whom we should love.

If, then, He led the children of Israel from the bondage of Egypt, we today can know that fact only if He Himself has told us. It is nothing more than folly to talk about what the Israelites may or may not have inferred from the events of the Exodus, unless those inferences were in accordance with the truth. The question is not whether the Israelites or some part of them were once in Egypt and then came out of Egypt. That question is comparatively unimportant. The question is whether, in fact, the God of the Hebrews did bring them out of Egypt and whether they were correct in their belief that He had so brought them out.

From the events themselves, it would not have been possible for the Israelites to learn much about the workings of God. The events of the Exodus were revelatory of God's power, but such revelation cannot properly be understood unless it also be accompanied by a revelation in words. We are living in a day that depreciates word-revelation, but, despite that fact, word-revelation is all-important. The Israelites realized that God was delivering them because God told them that it was so. Without a special communication from God to man, man cannot properly recognize or interpret the workings of God in history.

It is objected that if we approach the question of Old Testament theology, already having adopted theistic presuppositions, we are reasoning in a circle. We know how we shall come out even before we begin. We have, in such an event, excluded all scientific study. Frequent as is this charge, it is one which need not deter us. There can be no proper study of Old Testament theology apart from a consideration of Christian-theistic presuppositions. Indeed,

Old Testament theology can have validity only on such a foundation. To make such an assertion, however, brings with it the charge of reasoning in a circle.

The best way to meet this charge is to answer it head-on. Nothing is gained by evasion. And certainly nothing is to be gained by denying the charge. To deny the charge would simply bring on greater difficulty. If Christian theism undergirds a person's thinking, he will reason in a circle. He will see all truth in the light of God's truth. He will see light in God's light. Our final persuasion that the Scriptures are the Word of God is the inward testimony of the Holy Spirit, and, being persuaded of the Divine origin of Scripture, we accept what the Scripture says as the very Word of God. This is surely reasoning in a circle.

For our part, we do not see how it is possible to reason in any other way. All men, in so far as they act in consistency with their basic presuppositions, reason in a circle. And all men, whether consciously or not, have basic presuppositions. A man, for example, who starts with the presupposition, whether consciously adopted or not, that the Bible is not a special revelation of God, will arrive at conclusions which are consonant with his starting point and basic presuppositions. He is reasoning in a circle. As R. J. Rushdoony has so aptly stated, "All reasoning is circular reasoning, but reasoning from God to God-given and God-created data has the validity of conformity to the nature of things. The opponents of inspiration reason from autonomous man's reasons, through brute factuality which has no meaning other than man's interpretation, back again to man's basic presupposition. In other words, all reasoning moves in terms of its basic presupposition, either God or autonomous man, interpreting all reality in terms of the presupposition."[26]

We need not fear, then, if the charge of reasoning in a circle be raised. It is the only way in which one can legi-

26

timately reason. If, therefore, we accept the presuppositions of Christian theism, we shall see that the living and true God did intervene in human history and that He performed mighty acts for the redemption of mankind.

Suppose, however, that we reject the theistic presuppositions which are necessary for any proper study of Old Testament theology. Suppose we limit our inquiry to the study of that which ancient Israel believed about God and His dealings with herself. We approach with the principles of Form Criticism and we soon pare away the so-called editorial and interpretative accretions. We use the method of traditio-historical criticism to arrive at what we believe Israel herself had to say about her God, Yahweh. What is the result? When we have finally discovered the supposed *Sitz im Leben*, what have we accomplished? We have not come to grips with the basic question, namely, whether the result of our inquiry presents what, in fact, occurred, or simply what someone, somewhere along the line in Israel's history, thought may have happened. A true Old Testament theology must come to grips with the problem of revelation, and, when that is done, it will see that God did indeed intervene in a special way in the history of His people, Israel.

There is, then, a sense in which we may legitimately use and should use the word *Heilsgeschichte*, for there is a true history of salvation. But it should be noted that there cannot very well be a history of salvation unless there is first of all a salvation accomplished, and if there is a salvation accomplished there must also have been something from which man was saved. A true *Heilsgeschichte* will study the history of God's dealings with man which had to do with bringing man into a right relationship with God Himself. But such a concept is almost devoid of meaning, unless it be placed against the dark background of man's sin. Man is a sinner, and that is tantamount to saying that he is a

27

fallen creature. Old Testament theology, therefore, is concerned with, and deals with, the revelation of God as to what He has done for the redemption of man. Had man not been estranged from God by the Fall, and consequently a sinner, there would have been no need for Old Testament theology. Indeed, there would have been no such discipline as Old Testament theology.

When man first disobeyed God and fell into sin, there were overtures of grace on God's part. Even in the Garden of Eden it was revealed that that which would restore right relations between God and man was of grace. God did not say to the man and the woman, "Be at enmity with the serpent," but rather He declared, "And I will put enmity . . .". The remainder of the Old Testament records how God carried out His purpose of bringing about that the enmity which He had placed between the woman and the serpent should finally break out into that great conflict wherein the seed of the woman would bruise the serpent's head, and, in so doing, would Himself be wounded as to the heel. God called Abram from Ur of the Chaldees, and He led His people from Egyptian bondage and brought them into the land of promise; He gave them prophet, priest and king, until in the fullness of time He sent forth His Son.

What, then, is Old Testament theology? In the light of what we have previously been saying, it will be apparent that our definition is based upon Christian-theistic presuppositions. The word theology, according to its etymology, is simply the doctrine of God. Hence, we would define Old Testament theology as the study of God in His self-revelation in the Old Testament. In the study of Old Testament theology, therefore, we are basically concerned with a study of God Himself. From our study we should come to know more of Him. It goes without saying that we cannot study God apart from His revelation of Himself, and in this particular study it is that revelation which God once gave to mankind which we today denominate the Old Testament. Unless we are studying God Himself in His self-revelation, we are not studying theology.

It is clear from the Old Testament that God did, indeed, visit His people, and that these visitations took place in history. God met Moses, for example, at the burning bush, and as we study this revelation we shall be concerned to know all that the Scripture has to say about it.

Old Testament theology, therefore, must be based upon patient grammatico-historical exegesis. And if our study is truly theological, it will be more concerned with God than with Moses. What, indeed, may we say about Moses on this particular occasion? He approached the burning bush apparently out of idle curiosity; He had seen a bush burning and the bush was not consumed, and that was most unusual. What was the cause of it? "I will now turn aside, and see this great sight, why the bush is not burnt". (Exodus iii, 3) Other than that, we do not know what was in Moses' mind. After God had revealed Himself, then Moses hid his face, for He feared to look upon God. In that act we may learn something of Moses' understanding of the situation. It was the response of a man who had heard the true God speak to him. He was in the presence of God, and, therefore, like the seraphim in the Temple, he, too, would hide his face. The action showed that Moses recognized the holiness of God. "The place whereon thou standest is holy ground", he had been told. A true revelation had been given to him, and consequently he knew that he was in the presence of the true God. His action also showed that he considered himself a sinful and unworthy man, one who could not stand before God.

In saying what we have about Moses, it is clear that we have proceeded upon the assumption that, in what it says, the Scripture is trustworthy. Consequently, we have assumed that Moses did, indeed, act as the Scripture says he acted. But our study of Moses' response to God's revelation is not the principal content of the study of Old Testament theology. What is far more important than Moses' reaction or response to a revelation is the revelation itself. And this leads us to ask the question, How did God appear unto Moses? Why did He appear in the burning bush and as the Angel of the Lord? How did He identify Himself to Moses? What was the content of the revelation which He gave to Moses? The study of these questions is the subject-matter with which Old Testament theology at this particular stage is compelled to deal. But underlying all of this is the fact that must be faced—did this revelation take place in history or are we, after all, merely dealing with an aetiological story or saga, which later scribes for one reason or another have written down? And if the latter be so, are there different strands of tradition embedded in this narrative as we now have it?

It is at this particular point that a truly Scriptural Old Testament theology will part company with those approaches which do not receive the Scriptures as the authoritative revelation of God. If our study is to be truly biblical, it must come to grips with the fact that God—the living and true God, the triune God—did in fact reveal Himself to Moses at the burning bush. The revelation took place in history. It took place on a certain day of our calendar and at a very definite spot in the Sinai wilderness. There was a man named Moses, and there was a specific bush. The bush burned with fire, but, unlike other bushes which burn, this particular bush did not burn up, and the reason for this strange phenomenon was that God performed a miracle. Unless these historical facts are presupposed, we shall waste our time if we try to study the significance and meaning of what is narrated.

A proper study of Old Testament theology will be

deeply concerned with the significance and meaning of the episode. It will desire to ascertain where this particular revelation fits into God's covenantal dealings with His people, where it applies in the history of redemption. It will desire to see where this revelation belongs in a true *Heilsgeschichte*. For there is a true *Heilsgeschichte*. It is history such as that which Stephen summarized in his speech. It is a history of God's revelations unto His people and of His encounters with them. It is a history which will glorify and exalt God as the Creator and Sovereign over all. But it is history, history that took place upon this earth.

It is necessary today to stress the importance of history. Remove from it its historical basis and there is no true Christianity. For the Christian religion is founded squarely upon certain things which God did in history. Remove from it its historical basis and there can be no true study of Old Testament theology. When, however, proper regard is given to the historical basis of special revelation, how rewarding is the study of Old Testament theology! How wondrous were those dealings of God with His ancient people! How gracious were His overtures unto them! Step by step He brought them on their way, ever revealing unto them more about the One who was to come, until, in the fullness of time, God entered the realm of human history in a unique way. He sent forth His Son, and the second Person of the Trinity became man. To Him the kings, and priests, and prophets of the Old Testament dispensation pointed. And in Him was the fulfilment, for He was the true Prophet, the true Priest, and the true King, and it was He who by a definite act in history, namely, His atoning death and resurrection, healed the breach between man and God and brought salvation to His people.

NOTES TO LECTURE I

1. Cf. Young: *Thy Word Is Truth*, Grand Rapids, 1957, pp. 196–8.
2. Adolph Harnack: *What Is Christianity?* 1904. This is an English translation of *Das Wesen des Christentums*, which has recently been republished, Ehrenfried Klotz Verlag, Stuttgart, 1950.
3. Julius Wellhausen: *Prolegomena zur Geschichte Israels*, Berlin, 1905.
4. Albrecht Ritschl: *Die Christliche Lehre von der Rechtfertigung und Versöhnung*, 1874.
5. Alexander Pope: *Essay on Man*, Epistle III.
6. Form Criticism seeks to discover the original situation (*Sitz im Leben*) in which each individual unit of narrative, prophecy, poetry, etc., in the Old Testament arose. It does this by a removal of any editorial or secondary accretions. It then attempts to analyse and to classify the original units. Such a method of study can very easily become subjective and lead to scepticism.
7. Cf. *The Old Testament and Modern Study*, ed. H. H. Rowley, Oxford, 1951, for an up-to-date survey of modern views. See also H. A. Hahn, *The Old Testament in Modern Research*, Philadelphia, 1954. For a survey of recent Bible-believing scholarship in the field of the Old Testament, cf. Young, *The Old Testament*, in "Contemporary Evangelical Thought", Great Neck, New York, 1957, pp. 11–39.
8. Gerhard Von Rad: *Theologie des Alten Testaments*, Band 1, *Die Theologie der geschichtlichen Überlieferungen Israels*, München, 1957.
9. Von Rad: *op. cit.*, p. 7.
10. Johann Philipp Gabler: *De justo discrimine theologiae biblicae et dogmaticae recundisque recte utriusque finibus*, Altorfil, 1787.
11. Von Rad: *op. cit.*, pp. 14 ff.
12. *Idem*, pp. 23, 113.
13. *Idem*, p. 16.
14. J. Gresham Machen: *History and Faith*, in "The Princeton Theological Review", Vol. XIII, July, 1915.
15. J. C. K. von Hofmann: *Weissagungen und Erfüllungen im Alten Testament und Neuen Testament*, Vols. 1, 2, 1841, 1844.
16. Karl Barth: *Kirchliche Dogmatik*, IV: II, pp. 118–12; IV: I, pp. 331, 333, 377.
17. G. Ernest Wright: *God Who Acts*, London, 1952.
18. *Idem*, p. 11.
19. *Idem*, p. 13.

20. The English reader will find the text of Hattusilis's Apology in Sturtevant and Bechtel: *A Hittite Chrestomatly*, Philadelphia, 1935, pp. 42–83. These opening lines are significant. Cf., e.g., Virgil's Arma virumaque cano, *Aeneid*, I, 1.
21. *Op. cit.*, 1, 20.
22. *Idem*, 1, 39–58.
23. *Idem*, 2, 24.
24. *Idem*, 3, 1–12.
25. *Idem*, 4, 24–79.
26. R. J. Rushdoony, in a review of R. Laird Harris's *Inspiration and Canonicity*, which appeared in "Christianity Today", Vol. I, No. 19, June 24, 1957, p. 36.

Lecture II

THE NATURE OF OLD TESTAMENT
THEOLOGY

THE study of Old Testament theology, as we have sought
to stress in the last lecture, must be based upon a proper
concept of history, and there can be no proper concept of
history apart from presuppositions based upon Christian
theism. God did, in fact, intervene in human history in a
special way, in order that by means of His great saving
acts He might deliver mankind from the guilt and the
bondage of its sin.

At this stage, however, an objection is likely to arise.
We must not, it is objected, treat the Old Testament as
of one piece, turning now here and now there to find
statements about Christ and about Christian theology.
Criticism has been made of the *Christology of the Old Testament* by Hengstenberg, to the effect that Hengstenberg
finds Christian theology everywhere in the Old Testament. He treats every passage of the Old Testament, so it
is objected, as on a level with every other passage, and he
reads the doctrines of Christianity into passages which
originally had nothing to do with Christ.[1] It will be
remembered that Hengstenberg, like the Roman Catholic
scholar Reinke,[2] sought to trace throughout the Old Testament the development of the doctrine of the Messiah. He
studied the Messianic prophecies, one by one, and en-
deavoured to point out how they set forth the promise
that the Messiah should come.

Before we can properly consider such criticism, however, we must determine what kind of a book the Bible is.

34

If the Bible is not a revelation from God, in the sense traditionally maintained by the Church, and what is of infinitely more importance, in the sense which the Bible itself claims, then we cannot find Christ in the Old Testament at all. If the Bible is, after all, not a special revelation from God, but is nothing more than the religious writings of spiritually-gifted men of antiquity, we cannot expect to find Christ therein, in the sense that there are direct, predictive prophecies of Him.

(a) The Progressive Character of Old Testament Revelation

The question whether Hengstenberg, for example, finds Christ in the Old Testament is one which can truly be answered only upon the foundational presuppositions of Christian theism. Such criticism, however, will serve to enable us to bring to the fore, more clearly and pointedly an aspect of the genuine nature of biblical theology, namely, its progressive character. The first two verses of the Epistle to the Hebrews well set forth the true character of Old Testament theology, "God, who at sundry times and in divers manners spake in time past unto the fathers by the prophets, Hath in these last days spoken unto us by his Son, whom he hath appointed heir of all things, by whom also he made the worlds". (Heb. i, 1, 2) In these two verses a great contrast is presented. On the one hand, we are told that in the last days God has spoken in a Son. It is a final, completed, revelation. Before it, however, there was another, a revelation given through the prophets, and this previous revelation was given at sundry times and in divers manners. It was a revelation which prepared for, and pointed to, the final revelation to be given in a Son. In another passage of Hebrews this former revelation is characterized in the following words, "And Moses verily was faithful in all his house, as a servant, for a testimony of those things which were to be spoken after." We need not, however, depend upon the New Testament for statements to the effect that the revelation of the Old Testament was progressive. The Old Testament itself bears witness to this progression in revelation. Not inappropriately is the first book of the Bible named Genesis. It is truly a book of beginnings, and the later truths of the Bible are herein revealed in germ form. As we read through the history of the chosen people, we learn more and more about the purposes which God had for them and about the redemption which He intended to accomplish for them.

It is true that God could have given His completed revelation to man at one time, had He so desired. He is an omnipotent God and is not subject to man. Nevertheless, in His wisdom, He chose to give His saving revelation in progressive stages. There are a few verses in Scripture which enable us to understand, at least to an extent, why He chose to do this. In Hosea xi, 1, we read, "When Israel was a child, then I loved him, and called my son out of Egypt," and in verse three, "I taught Ephraim also to go, taking them by their arms; but they knew not that I healed them." In Acts xvii, 30, it is stated, "And the times of this ignorance God winked at; but now commandeth all men everywhere to repent." And again, "He saith unto them, Moses because of the hardness of your hearts suffered you to put away your wives: but from the beginning it was not so". (Matthew xix, 8)

These verses will, at least, give us a clue to the reason why God gave man a progressive revelation. For one thing, man was not ready to receive a full revelation until the proper time had come and God was ready to give such a revelation. It may be difficult for us to grasp this. Could not the fallen Adam, for example, have understood the full revelation of the saving work of Christ as well as, let us say, the Apostle Paul? In the wisdom of God, however, fallen man was not ready for this completed revelation until the New Testament age had begun to run its course. By long training and preparation Israel had to be brought to the stage where she could truly recognize her sin and her need for salvation. Then again, this long period of preparation was one in which the lovingkindness and patience of God were manifested. The Bible stresses God's forbearance. He would restrain His hand of punishment, in order that man might repent, for He delights not in the death of the sinner.[3]

At any rate, whether we today may fully understand the reasons for the method of revelation which God has chosen, sufficient has been revealed in the Old Testament to make it clear that it was for man's benefit, and also to show forth the forbearance of God and so to exalt Him, that He communicated His truth to man in the manner in which He did.

From the very beginning it was made clear to man that God would do something to heal the breach between God and man which sin had introduced. As the days passed, further information as to God's purposes was communicated to man. That, in barest essentials, is what is meant by progressive revelation. It is the progressive unfolding of the plan of God in the salvation of sinners.

It would follow, therefore, that Abraham and Moses, for example, did not have the full knowledge of the purposes of God which was the possession of the saints of God who lived during the days of the apostles. We cannot, as a consequence, expect to find a fully-developed presentation of Christian truth in the Old Testament, such as we find in the New. The fact is obvious, and, as far as is known, it has been acknowledged by Christians throughout the ages. We need but think of the expression attributed to Augustine,

> *The New is in the Old concealed,*
> *The Old is in the New revealed.*[4]

With this recognition, therefore, of the progressive nature of Old Testament revelation, we must avoid the pitfall of reading into the texts of the Old Testament what is not to be found there. That would be to fail to do justice to this very progressive character of revelation. At the same time, it is also necessary to insist, particularly in these days, that whereas the revelation of the Old Testament was progressive, it was also genuine revelation. Its source is the same ever-living and blessed God who spoke to the apostles. It was, to be sure, at sundry times and in divers manners that God spoke, but it was God who spoke. The truth which God made known to the fathers may have been partial and preparatory; it may have lacked the fullness of the New Testament revelation, but it was truth. What God said about Himself to Moses does not conflict with what He said about Himself to John. There is no room for Marcionism in a true Old Testament theology. The Old Testament revelation required supplementation, but it did not require correction. It was not erroneous, it was not the communication of information about God and His purposes which was not true. It was, indeed, a partial and incomplete revelation, but it was a revelation.

(b) Revelation in Epochs

As we read the pages of the Old Testament, we notice that it divides the history of the chosen race into what we may term epochs or periods of revelation. This is the second important characteristic of Old Testament theology, namely, that it recognizes these great outsanding epochs of revelation. We can determine these epochs and their relation to one another only from the Old Testament itself. The Scriptures alone can tell us what these epochs are and how they are to be identified.

The study of Scripture leads us to identify an epoch as a particular period in the history of Israel which sustained a unique relation to the plan of God in redemption. For example, the Scriptures regard the period of the patriarchs as unique. This period follows after that described in Genesis i-xi, and it prepares for the time of Egyptian bondage. During this period God revealed Himself to individuals, known as patriarchs, by means of visions, dreams, theophanies and the Angel of the Lord. A common designation of God during this period, particularly when the patriarchs were in need of assurance of God's omnipotence, was the term *El Shaddai*. This period thus stands out by itself as a unique epoch of divine revelation.

It must be stressed that the essence or character of divine revelation was the same in all these periods of Israel's history. In every epoch it is the same God who speaks to Israel or to her ancestors, and in every epoch the revelation is genuinely revelation. It would be unbiblical to equate revelation with man's understanding of the truth. It is possible that, because of the sinfulness of his heart, man at times entertained incorrect notions of the nature of God. But the Old Testament says surprisingly little about what man thought about God. A careful study of the Old Testament will, it is true, enable us to learn to a certain extent how man reacted toward's God's revelation, and for the most part we are told that the ancient Israelites were a sinful, stubborn, hard-hearted, recalcitrant nation, which engaged in a constant practical atheism. They acted as though they did not believe that God existed. But the emphasis of the Old Testament is not upon what man thought about God; it is upon what God made known to man, and such communication of knowledge upon God's part alone is true and genuine revelation.

If the essential nature of revelation itself does not change, the method in which revelation is communicated does, indeed, vary. It may very well be that the reason for this is to be found in the stage of preparation of the recipient for such revelation. Before the Fall there was special revelation, for God spoke directly to Adam. And in the period before the patriarchs there were also direct communications to man on God's part. During the time of the patriarchs, however, there was more variety in revelation, at least, more variety is recorded. With the period of the bondage in Egypt we are introduced to the first great period of miracles in Israel's history. At this time the Lord showed His sovereignty over the forces of nature which He had created, and He also manifested His power over the false gods of Egypt in the performance of many mighty miracles.

We must note also the revelation given in the events at Sinai with the tremendous theophanies which occurred there. Likewise, we must note the pillar of cloud and of fire. Then, as we follow the Israelites into the land of promise, we must note the fulfilment of the earlier promises in the raising up of the institutions of prophecy and kingship. The priesthood itself, with the tabernacle and its sacrifices, was also a revelation of the will of God. It was in the ministry of the prophets, however, that God gave to Israel that wonderful body of predictions which we know as the Messianic prophecies. Throughout the course of her history God did, indeed, speak to Israel at sundry times and in divers manners, yet it was one and the same God who spoke, and His messages were genuine communications to His people.

In thus mapping out the field of revelation and considering the various epochs which constituted the period of God's revelation to His people in Old Testament times, we must also, if we wish properly to engage in the study of Old Testament theology, do justice to the distinction which the Bible makes between the pre- and the postlapsarian periods. There was a time, according to the Bible, when man was holy, free from sin, and in perfect communion with God. It was the time of man's innocency. The state of innocency, the Bible tells us, has been lost because of man's disobedience. Any proper study of Old Testament theology will pay due heed to this all-important distinction.

In recent times many attempts have been made to avoid the clear-cut teaching of the Bible on this. It is not necessary, nor is there time, at this juncture, to mention all these attempts. On the one hand, there are those who say that these early chapters of Genesis belong to the realm of *Heilsgeschichte*, and that the events which they describe are not events which took place here upon this earth but rather are events which belong to the spiritual world.[5] Others regard these early chapters of Genesis as parables, intended merely to teach a lesson.[6] Adam is every man, we are told, or Adam is ourselves. Yet others reject this view and claim that the experiences related of Adam are the experiences of ourselves. They teach that man once was an unfallen creature and they are intended to explain the entrance of sin into the world.[7]

It is a temptation today to adopt the view that we must rethink the interpretation of these early chapters of Genesis. It is true that there are accounts of creation among other nations. Must we, then, be greatly influenced in our interpretation of Genesis by the accounts which other nations have left us? We must study these other documents, but they are in no sense to be the standards which must guide our interpretation of Genesis. Genesis is the Word of God, and our primary task is to learn what it has to say. It is not a document similar to other documents which have come down to us from the ancient Near East. It is a special revelation of God Himself, and if we deny or obscure or minimize this fact, we shall never properly understand Genesis. This is not to say that we cannot learn from the other documents of antiquity. We can, indeed, learn from them, and in some respects we can greatly profit by their study, but in the interpretation of Genesis we shall be far more greatly benefited by a study of what Paul had to say in Romans v, for example, than by a minute comparison of Genesis with *Enuma Elish*[8] or by an attempt to discover the "genre" of Genesis as a document from the ancient Near East.

True Old Testament theology, therefore, must do full justice to the fact of the Fall. It must study pre-lapsarian revelation in order to learn of God's goodness to man in his unfallen state, but it must also pay due heed to the fact that post-lapsarian revelation can be understood only as it is based upon the supposition that man is a fallen creature, and that the once harmonious relation between God and man has been ruptured by man's sin. At the same time, post-lapsarian revelation is anticipatory and preparatory, for it points forward and also looks forward to the time when God will send the seed of the woman to bruise the serpent's head and so to restore right relations between God and man.

Old Testament theology, therefore, must take the Bible seriously. In saying this we wish to make ourselves as clear as possible. There are those today who say that we must become more biblical in our thinking. One of the charges sometimes brought against conservatives, for example, is that they should become more biblical.[9] If by such a charge it was intended that we should pay more heed to the infallible authority and truthworthiness of Scripture in all our thinking and practice, we should have nothing but sympathy for this charge. In this sense, we should all strive to be more biblical. Is this, however, the sense in which the charge is often made? We fear not; we fear that today this charge implies something different. For, when the word "biblical" is thus employed, it is not used to suggest that we should simply regard the Bible as true and

trustworthy in all that it says. The word today is sometimes used in a different sense to suggest that we should
regard the Bible as did the ancient Hebrews. They saw the
mighty works of God and learned of Him from His works.
They were not interested in propositional revelation; they
were interested in a dynamic, vital, living faith. Apparently, they had no time for a static, dead revelation, but
they believed in the living God. Our conservative way of
looking at the Bible, we are told, is in fact rationalistic. It
is based upon Aristotle, and while it may be satisfactory
for students of twentieth-century science, it is not the mode
of thought which we find in the Bible itself. The categories
of causality, for example, are not satisfactory for setting
forth a doctrine of creation, and, for that reason, mytho-
logical language is employed. This, it is claimed, is biblical, and when we are told that we must be more biblical,
what is really meant, it would seem, is that we must give
up once and for all the doctrine of the plenary and verbal
inspiration of the Bible.

It is not in this modern sense, then, that Old Testament
theology must take the Bible seriously. For the modern
idea of what is "biblical" is based upon the dialecticism
and existentialism which are so rampant in our day. There
is, however, a proper sense in which we must be truly
biblical in our study of Old Testament theology. We must
take the Bible seriously as the authoritative Word of God.
We must pay due heed to its trustworthiness. Indeed, the
discipline of Old Testament theology cannot consistently
be carried on in conjunction with a refusal to take the
statements of the Bible as authoritative. To cite an example, if the method of documentary analysis now in
vogue and the tenets of Form Criticism are legitimate
ways of biblical study, there can then, in all consistency,
be no proper study of Old Testament theology.

If the Bible is the Word of God, it follows that all that

the Bible says is true and authoritative, and only when the Bible's statements are thus regarded will it be possible to study what God has said to man. Admittedly, Old Testament theology regards the Bible as a revelation from God to man. Much recent study of the subject, however, does not do justice to this aspect of the Bible, namely, its Divine character as revelation. Our principal criticism of Von Rad's latest work, for example, is that it is not Old Testament theology.[10] We greatly admire the scholarship which underlies the book, and we also admire the clear manner in which the author has presented his material. Despite its title, however, *Theologie des Alten Testaments*, the work is not a theology of the Old Testament. If, as Von Rad asserts, we are to study only what Israel herself, in one way or another, had to say about what she thought God (Yahweh) had done for her, we are not studying theology. If we assume that the framework of the Hexateuch, for example, has given us an incorrect picture of the early history of Israel, and that about the only thing which we can positively assert concerning the ancestors of Israel in the pre-Mosaic or patriarchal period is that they engaged in that form of worship which the late Albrecht Alt called the worship of the "God of the fathers",[11] we have, in reality, expressed a scepticism concerning the early books of the Bible which precludes any proper study of theology.

(c) Messianic Prophecy

It is true that there is a human side to the Bible. God gave us this book, but He employed human penmen in its composition. These human writers of the Scriptures wrote in the language of the people among whom they lived, and they employed the modes of expression and forms of thought which were common to the people of their time. They were in no sense mere automata, but rather men whose personalities and gifts were brought into the fullest

44

play in the writing of the Scriptures. In His providence God had prepared just those men whom He desired to be the penmen of His Word and upon them He brought the superintendence of His Spirit, so that they wrote precisely what He wished to have written. Nevertheless, they were men; holy men, indeed, but men of their time. God did not give His revelation in a vacuum. He gave it in the language and in the modes of expression that would be understood by those who received it. There is, therefore, a very genuine and proper sense in which it may be said that the Bible is an oriental book. And, inasmuch as it is an oriental book, one who would properly study it must know something of that cultural *milieu* in which the Bible appeared among men. He must know the languages of the Bible and of the peoples who lived about the children of Israel. It is difficult to over-emphasize the importance of archaeology to biblical study. To be sure, what we are to believe about God and what duty God has required of us, can be learned from the Bible even by the ignorant. But for the full study of Scripture, we must do full justice to the fact that God gave this message of salvation in a certain very definite cultural *milieu*.

This very fact, however, raises a problem. Because the Bible bears a formal similarity to other literatures of antiquity, there are some who would conclude that the Bible therefore derived its content entirely from these other literatures. The pan-Babylonian school of Delitzsch and Winckler was an extreme example of this, but it is difficult to escape the conclusion that, even today, there are those who, in effect, at least, are reviving some of the tenets of that school. They are attempting to explain the Bible as a book the contents of which were simply derived, for the most part, from the peoples round about Israel. A recent illustration of this tendency may be seen in the attempts which some have made to explain some of the distinctive contents of Christianity as having come from Qumran.[12]

We can perhaps best understand the relationship which the Bible sustains to the cultures that surrounded Israel by the consideration of a few examples. There is the vision of Isaiah. Is this an inaugural call to the prophetic ministry, or is it rather a vision designed to prepare the prophet for a specific ministry? For the present purpose, it does not matter particularly which one of these views we adopt, but there is good reason for considering it to be the vision which Isaiah received when he was inaugurated in the prophetic ministry.

In this vision mention is made of the temple, the *hekal*, and consequently, the vision has sometimes been regarded as having cultic connotations. There are other reasons also given for assuming that the vision has cultic associations, such as the purification of the lips of the prophet, the opening of the mouth, the sending forth of a messanger, the prayer of intercession, the mention of the teil and terebinth tree, which has been thought to be a reflexion upon the tree of life. Likewise, it is claimed that the language of the chapter contains some of the technical terms of the cult, namely, the usage of the verb *qārā'* in the sense *to chant*, the term *qôdesh*, *holiness*, and the contrast with impurity, the reference to glory and to the filling of the temple, the expression "how long", and the thought of sin being expiated.[13]

There are some, such as the late Professor Bentzen, who would go beyond this and claim that we have in Isaiah vi a passage representing the festival of the ascension of the throne of Yahweh.[14] The king has ascended the throne, he says, and remains there as God's king. With respect to this whole idea of divine kingship in Israel and the festival of the ascension of the throne (*Thronbesteigungsfest*), it should be noted that there is no reference to such a festival in the

Bible. Rather, the Lord (Yahweh) is represented as having always been king; He does not become king. He is praised and honoured because He is the king, but never, despite some attempts to make it appear so, is He praised because He has just become king. The renewal of His kingship was not, as far as we know from the Bible, an object of celebration among the ancient Hebrews.

It should further be noted that in ancient Israel there were no celebrations held in which Yahweh's supposed victories over the dragon of chaos or other monsters were celebrated. What was celebrated, however, and what was emphasized, was the wondrous deliverance that the Lord wrought when He brought His people out of the land of Egypt. In the Psalms we find confession of individual sins and also of the sins of the people, acknowledgment of the Lord's many mercies and of the evidences of His goodness, together with prayer and praise and adoration of the Lord's Holy Name. This worship of the Lord, however, is concerned with historical events. The Psalmist rejoices because God has delivered His people, or has intervened in their history. Furthermore, unlike the other nations of antiquity, the kingship of Yahweh was not tied up with the earthly kingship in such a sense that, if the earthly king perished, the kingship of Yahweh would also come to an end. The earthly kingship did, indeed, perish when the nation, because of its sins against Yahweh, was carried into captivity. The earthly kingship could thus change its character, but the kingship of Yahweh endured without change. Very clearly, the kingship of Yahweh was not grounded upon the earthly kingship. If anything, the earthly king, as with Saul, sometimes took unto himself prerogatives which belonged to Yahweh alone. The earthly king was to be a representative of the divine king, one who would so administer the kingdom with justice and judgment that the Lord, Yahweh of Hosts, would be glorified in the hearts of the people, and they, because of the human government, administered in the name of the Lord, would walk in His statutes and obey His laws.

We may, therefore, dismiss the idea once and for all that in Isaiah vi we have any appearance of the idea of divine kingship, such as it manifested itself in a festival of a god's ascension of the throne. To treat the chapter in such a way is to miss the seriousness with which it presents its message.

For this reason, we shall not devote more attention to the thought that Isaiah vi is related to the festival of the king's ascension of the throne. It is necessary, however, to consider more carefully the claim that this chapter relates events which have a distinctly cultic reference. There will be no need to consider every suggested point of reference, but, at least, we may reflect upon a few. We may briefly consider the purification of the lips, and the opening of the mouth. With respect to the seraph flying to Isaiah and touching his lips we read, "And he laid *it* upon my mouth, and said, Lo, this hath touched thy lips; and thine iniquity is taken away, and thy sin purged." (Isaiah vi, 7) This act is sometimes regarded as a rite of purification similar to rites of Mesopotamia and Egypt.[15]

There are certain rites in the ancient worship of Mesopotamia to which appeal has been made as a proper background for the understanding of Isaiah vi. In the house of ablution, the *bit rimki*, the mouth was washed with lustral water. It was the function of the king to wash the mouth and to open the mouth of statues of gods which were being delivered to the cult.[16] Among the Hittites also, when people became reconciled to one another, the mouth and tongue were purified.[17] In Egypt the mouth of a corpse in the ritual of the dead was touched with sharp instruments, such as knives, and was painted with nitrate and perfumed.[18]

In the rhetorical question of the Lord and in the sending forth of a messenger, we are told that there is also present the influence of a widespread ancient oriental cult. Stress has been placed upon the plural which is used by the Lord, "Who will go for us?" As in the vision of Micaiah, the son of Imlah, so here also, it is claimed, the reference is to the heavenly court. Micaiah saw the Lord seated upon His throne, and all the host of heaven was standing by Him, on His right hand and on His left. The Lord called for a messenger who would go forth and deceive Ahab, and such a messenger was found and sent. So also, it is claimed, in the vision of Isaiah we have to do with the heavenly court. In an Akkadian text the god of heaven, Anu, addresses the priest, Ashipu. He asks, "Whom shall I send?" From this it is thought that in the question of the Lord we are to see a particular formula.

Another feature will also be of interest. In response to the Lord's question and commission, Isaiah asks, "How long, O Lord?" Attention has been directed to the use of the phrase *adi mati* (how long?) on Akkadian texts. Thus, we may note the following lines from an Assyrian supplication:

> *How long, O my Lord,*
> *will mine enemies cast evil glances at me . . .*
> *How long, O my Lord,*
> *will the miserable lillu come towards me . . .*
> *How long, O my Lord,*
> *Art thou enangered, and is thy visage turned away?*
> *How long, O my Lord,*
> *Art thou angry and thy soul in anger? (furious)*
> *Turn thy neck toward him whom thou hast rejected*
> *For a word of grace, set thy face.*[19]

There is a Babylonian ritual by the name of *surpa* (burning, passion, ardour), a ritual which has to do with the expiation of sin. The Hebrews, also, it has been claimed, knew of the transforming power of fire. But can it be said that it is the fire itself which purifies the lips of Isaiah? Is not the fire, rather, merely symbolical of the fact that the prophet's sins have been expiated?

The few examples which have just been adduced serve to drive home the point that God did not give His revelation to the prophet in a *milieu* that the prophet would not understand. It is perfectly true, and the fact cannot be denied, that there are formal similarities in the language and in the content of the vision of Isaiah with certain rites and rituals of the ancient oriental world. A proper study of Old Testament theology should certainly acknowledge this fact, should take into account the discoveries of archaeology, and should also recognize the importance of a knowledge of the ancient cognate languages of Hebrew.

What, however, is to be our interpretation of these facts? Shall we conclude that, because certain terms of the ancient cults are found in Isaiah vi, the writer of Isaiah has been influenced by that ancient world of cults?

At this stage a proper study of Old Testament theology would cause the student to remember that the Bible is the Word of God, a true revelation from Him. He would note that the vision recorded in Isaiah vi was a genuine vision. God did, indeed, visit the prophet and communicated to him by means of a vision the message which He desired the prophet to have. The vision, therefore, was objective to Isaiah. It was not a product of his own mind, but was imposed upon him or granted to him from without by God. Inasmuch as it was a vision and the experiences described took place in a vision, we do not know whether it occurred in the earthly temple or not. We are not told the location in which the vision came to Isaiah. What is more important is that it was a true vision.

Inasmuch as it was a true vision, it contained a message for the prophet, and was therefore given to him in a form in which he could understand it. For that reason mention is made of the *hekal*, in order that the prophet should be reminded of the sacredness of the events. The same is true of the mention of an altar. By these facts Isaiah would be reminded of the earthly temple and would know that the message which he was to receive had come to him from the dwelling place of God Himself. It is also true that the language used was to a large extent that of cultic worship. How could it have been otherwise? Other cults also had altars; other cults also taught, at least in a formal manner, the expiation of sins; other cults had messengers of the god.

The same is true of the situation existing today. More than one religion has words for God, priest, temple, worship, sacrifice, prayer, missions. If one were to make a study of the subject, one would notice many formal similarities in the religious exercises of contemporary religions. It does not follow from this, however, that these religions are all of a piece. In the same manner, we may say that there was also a common vocabulary of religion and a formal similarity in religious practice in the ancient world. The vision granted to Isaiah, therefore, was such as he could understand, and for this reason was couched in the language in which it is actually found.

It is only when we consider the differences, however, that we can arrive at the truth. And the first difference that must be stressed is that the One in Isaiah's vision who sits upon the throne is the true King of kings and Lord of lords. We are not merely presented with a conception of Yahweh which was held by one of the best and most spiritually-discerning men of the eighth century B.C. We are given, rather, a revelation of the sovereign God, who in infinite condescension appeared in human form to the prophet. It may be that Anu is said to have asked,

"Whom shall I send?" The words, however, are meaningless, for Anu is a figment of the imagination of the sinful heart of man. But the One who in all solemnity asks, "Whom shall I send, and who will go for is?" is none other than the God whose glory is the fullness of all the earth.

It should also be noticed that when the seraph touches the lips of Isaiah, he is performing a symbolical act to show that the sins of the prophet have been removed. It is not merely the removal of ritual uncleanness; it is a sign that the sins which caused the prophet to cry out, "I am undone", have been removed.

This is far different from any rituals of purification of the mouth or lips which are found in Egypt or in Mesopotamia. The word *kipper* also has a significance in the Old Testament which can be paralleled nowhere in the religions of antiquity. In the Old Testament it has to do with the covering or expiation of sins committed against a holy God.[20] As to the mission of Isaiah, therefore, it cannot be compared with so-called "missions" of antiquity. Here is an asseveration upon the part of God, an asseveration which has to do with the eternal destinies of men. Isaiah goes forth not as a mere soothsayer or diviner, representing some local god, but he goes forth as a true messenger of the Lord of Hosts to preach a message which will affect the relationships that men sustain to this ever-living God. In any proper study of the passage, a true Old Testament theology will naturally pay full heed to every word and will note the usage of those words in other languages and cultures of the ancient world, but it will also at every stage keep in mind that the Bible is, after all, a revelation from God, and, consequently, it will seek to do justice to that fact in its interpretation of the passage.

In Isaiah xi, to give another example, the Messiah is set forth as One who will conquer all His enemies and rule the earth in righteousness. "And righteousness shall be the girdle of his loins, and faithfulness the girdle of his reins." (Isaiah xi, 5) What is the meaning of the figure of a girdle used in this particular verse? Commentators have advanced different explanations. It has been suggested (e.g. by Drechsler) that clothing indicates character or denotes the qualities of the wearer, and for that reason righteousness and faithfulness are here mentioned as the girdle which the Messiah wears. Another view is that the girdle was an essential part of the oriental dress, and that which kept the other clothing in its proper place. Still another view is that the girdle is the symbol of power (Duhm) or also royalty (Calvin). Kittel, in his revision of Dillmann, came near the truth when he suggested that the girdle might be a requirement of the warrior. He went on to suggest, however, that the Messiah was not a warrior, but the Prince of Peace.[21]

Archaeology has shed light on this mode of expression, and the language of Isaiah may now be clearly understood. It is, indeed, the figure of a warrior that is here presented. The Messiah is prepared for combat, and the weapons of His warfare and also the prize for which He contends is the girdle of righteousness and faithfulness. In so contending and bringing about the destruction of His enemies, He is at the same time acting as the Prince of Peace, for He is doing what is necessary to procure peace.

Belt- or girdle-wrestling was known in the ancient world.[22] This is seen, for example, by pictures from the tombs of Beni Hassan in Egypt.[23] The aim of the wrestling, at least in some instances, seems to have been to procure the belt of the opponent, and the one who procured the belt was regarded as the victor. There is also an attestation of this practice in the *Iliad* (23: 710) and the *Odyssey* (24: 89). We may note also the statue of the Khafaje wrestlers from the third millennium B.C. in Mesopotamia. Of unusual interest in this connection is a text from Nuzi in which the thought of belt- or girdle-wrestling is set forth as an ordeal in court.[24] According to this text, two brothers are involved in a suit at law. One of them, Matteshub, is accused by his brother, Gurpazah, of assaulting and injuring Gurpazah's wife. The accused denies the truthfulness of the accusation, and the judges prescribe as an ordeal a form of belt-wrestling. Gurpazah comes out the victor and is acquitted. We may render the pertinent portion of the text as follows:

"They said, 'Go! carry the gods to Matteshub! When Gurpazah goes to the gods, then Matteshub is to seize Gurpazah and he is to wrest (i.e., try to wrest) his belt in his belt. Gurpazah prevailed in the suit. And the judges sentenced Matteshub (that he should pay) one ox to Gurpazah for his belt."

It is evidently this conception which underlay the familiar expression, "to gird up one's loins", The belt or the girdle thus became the symbol of the warrior about to fight. Hence we may understand what lies behind the expression in Job "gird up thy loins now like a man: I will demand of thee, and declare thou unto me". (Job xl, 7; xxxviii, 3) In Isaiah's prophecy, we may then conclude, the Messiah is depicted as a warrior, One who will fight and One who is prepared for the fight. At this stage, therefore, we see that the language of the Bible uses a form of expression which was evidently current in the ancient world. The original force of the expression has been lost in the description, but Isaiah evidently desired to use language which would set forth the Messiah as one who was prepared for the conflict in order to establish His kingdom and to overcome all obstacles which should stand in the way of such preparation.

We may compare our own usage of such phrases as "when my ship comes home". In thus speaking, we are simply thinking of the time when we shall have made our fortune; we certainly have no reference to a literal ship. The same is true of Isaiah's usage. The original force of the phrase had probably disappeared from the language. Today, however, we know enough about that original force so that we may assert that it was Isaiah's intention to picture the Messiah in the rôle of a conqueror. We are not to interpret his mention of the girdle, therefore, as necessarily a sign of power or of royalty, or as merely indicating character or that part of the clothing which binds the rest and holds it together. Isaiah has chosen a form of statement which shows that the Messiah was a warrior, one who could face all of His foes and build up His kingdom without hindrance from any obstacle.

One or two more examples will suffice. In Genesis xiv we read of Melchizedek, who was priest of the most high God (*'El 'Elyôn*). (Genesis xiv, 18) It is well known that the designation *'El* was frequently employed in the literature of Ugarit. The principal god of the Ugaritic pantheon was *'El*. In the study of Old Testament theology how are we to interpret the statements which are made concerning *'El 'Elyôn,* the god whom Melchizedek served? It might be suggested that here was an old Canaanitish survival, and that there was no essential difference between the *'El 'Elyôn* of Melchizedek and the *'El* of ancient Canaan. But the traditional interpretation of this passage which has found acceptance in the Christian Church is doubtless correct, in seeing in the figure of Melchizedek one who had preserved the true religion, apart from the line of promise. When Melchizedek worshipped *'El 'Elyôn,* he was worshipping the supreme God, and Abram recognized that this was so. Melchizedek was worshipping the Creator of heaven and earth. Melchizedek, however, lived in Canaan, and he used the term *'El* to designate this God. That the Canaanites employed the same designation does not affect this picture.

We may note a modern parallel. The merest beginner in Arabic knows that the word *Allah* is constantly employed to designate the god of Islam. When the Bible was translated into Arabic, the word which the translators employed in order to designate the true God was also *Allah*. When a Moslem speaks of *Allah* he has one thing in mind; when a Christian speaks of Him, he has something else in mind. Both, however, use precisely the same word.

A proper study of Old Testament theology will show not only the similarities, but also the differences. The context in which the appearance of Melchizedek is related makes it clear that there was truly a spiritual bond between this king of Salem and priest of *'El 'Elyôn*, on the one hand, and Abram, the Hebrew, on the other. The king of Sodom is merely interested in the captives of war, but Melchizedek sought to provide refreshment for Abram's army and a spiritual blessing. Abram recognized a kinship, and accepted the blessing, in that he paid tithes to Melchizedek. It would certainly be difficult to imagine Abram giving such homage to a mere Canaanitish king and his gods. The very religion of Abram, if we take the Bible at face value, was a repudiation of the polytheism of Canaan. Yet, strangely enough, in the God of Melchizedek, Abram recognizes One to whom he might pay tithes.

The same approach may be employed with respect to Isaiah's words of annunciation in Isaiah vii, 14. Engnell has said that the language which the prophet uttered was a "divine-royal ($εὐαγγέλιον$) formula".[25] Similar language had been used at Ugarit.[26] The words occur:

$$\text{tld, btl (t}$$
$$\overline{\text{hl}} \ \overline{\text{glmt}} \ \text{tld b(n}$$

"A virgin will give birth . . . a damsel will bear a son." In the passage from Ugarit this language announces the birth of a child to the gods. In Scripture, however, such is not so. The formula is used of Ishmael and of Samson, as well as in the Messianic passage, Isaiah vii, 14. At the same time, it is not going too far to assert that the language always suggests the birth of some prominent person. It announces an unusual birth.

As we approach the study of this formula in Isaiah, we may do full justice to its ancient Near Eastern setting. We may recognize that there was doubtless a definite reason why the prophet employed these words. He must have known that they would have brought to the minds of his hearers certain very definite connotations. And for precisely that reason he employed them. As soon as an Israelite would hear this language, he would realize that an announcement of stupendous importance was about to be made.

We cannot, however, simply dismiss this by saying that the prophet has employed an oriental formula of birth-announcement. We cannot say merely that he was influenced by the culture of his times. We must examine his words on their own merit. We must consider them in the context in which they are found, nor have we the right by means of Form Criticism to remove this context. When we do approach these words we make the discovery that Isaiah is not speaking about the birth of some supposed son of the gods, nor is he simply employing the language of a well-known formula for his purpose, but rather, with all the earnestness that characterized one who had received his commission from the Lord Himself, He is announcing the coming of one whose name was to be called Immanuel, whose mother could be designated by the unusual word *almah* and the announcement of whose birth was so significant that it could be classed as a sign comparable to the signs which had been offered to Ahaz. In other words, when we take the Bible as it stands we are here face to face with a Messianic prophecy of wondrous beauty and significance.

The recognition of the oriental background of Scripture in no way detracts from the supernatural character of its message. God gave His special revelation to a people living in the midst of idolatry and superstition. He employed the forms of thought to which they were accustomed. He did not divorce His revelation from the background in which they were placed. He gave a Book that is truly human, but which in a far more profound sense is truly Divine. He gave His Word.

The study of Old Testament theology, therefore, if it is to do justice to the phenomena, will recognize the Scriptures as a special Divine revelation. It will operate upon the principles of Christian theism. It will also seek to do full justice to the character of special revelation as progressive. It will not seek to discover Christian doctrine where that doctrine is not to be found, but it will keep in mind the fact that all Scripture was spoken by the God of truth. It will, therefore, not shy away from this revelation, but will recognize that it is truly a preparation for the final revelation in Jesus Christ. Most earnestly, and based upon sober grammatico-historical exegesis, will it endeavour to do full justice to the progressive character of the Old Testament revelation.

It will also remember the great epochs of revelation, and, seeking to discover these epochs, will be guided alone by the Scriptures. And lastly, it will pay full heed to the words of the Bible and to the background against which these words were spoken.

Old Testament theology is a challenging study. It is particularly challenging in these days when so many mistake its essential nature and regard it merely as the study of what Israel thought or said about God. How all-important, then, that we devote our best energies to the exposition of the great truth that "God, who at sundry times and in divers manners spake in time past unto the fathers by the prophets, Hath in these last days spoken unto us by *his* Son". (Hebrews i, 1, 2a)

NOTES TO LECTURE II

1. E. W. Hengstenberg: *Christology of the Old Testament*. The work was re-issued in 1956. Dorner (*History of Protestant Theology*), Edinburgh, Vol. II, p. 436, remarks that Hengstenberg sought "to prove that those doctrines which are most peculiar to the New were already completed and established doctrines of the Old". Note his quotations from Oehler to the same effect. Cf. also T. K. Cheyne: *The Prophecies of Isaiah*, New York, 1881, pp. 280–1.

2. Laur. Reinke: *Die Messianischen Weissagungen bei den grossen und kleinen Propheten des A. T.*, Geisen., Vols. I–IV, 1859–1862.

3. Ezekiel xviii, 32.

4. Augustine: Quaestiones in *Heptateuchum*, II, lxxiii, in Migne, *Patrologia Latina*, Vol. xxxiv, col. 623, "Quanquam et in vetere novum lateat, et in novo vetus pateat."

5. This view has been ably expounded by Otto A. Piper: *God in History*, New York, 1939.

6. Alan Richardson: *Genesis I-XI*, 1953.

7. Gabriel Hebert: *Fundamentalism and the Church*, Philadelphia, 1957, p. 40.

8. Enuma Elish (when on high), the first two words of the Babylonian creation account. See Alexander Heidel: *The Babylonian Genesis*, Chicago, 1951.

9. Cf., e.g., what Hebert (*op. cit.*) has written, pp. 96–8.

10. Gerhard Von Rad: *Theologie des Alten Testaments*, München, 1957.

11. Albrecht Alt: *Der Gott der Väter*, Stuttgart, 1929.

12. E.g., by Edmund Wilson: *The Scrolls From the Dead Sea*, New York, 1955.

13. Cf. the recent discussion by Ph. Béguerie: "La Vocation d' Isaie", in *Etudes sur Les Prophètes d'Israel*, Paris, 1954.

14. Aage Bentzen: *Jesaja*, København, 1944, Vol. I, p. 47.

15. Cf. Béguerie: *op. cit.*, p. 27.

16. References in Béguerie: *op. cit.*, p. 28.

17. R. Dussaud: *Les religions des Hittites, des Pheniciens et des Syriens*, Paris, 1945, p. 349.

18. References in Béguerie: *op. cit.*, p. 27
19. Cf. Beguerie: *op. cit.*, p. 35. The text is found in Dhorme: *Choix de textes religieux Assyro-Babyloniens*, Paris, 1907, pp. 163–5.
20. Cf. Roger Nicole: *C. F. Dodd and the Doctrine of Propitiation*, Westminster Theological Journal, Vol. XVII, No. 2, pp. 117–57.
21. August Dillmann: *Der Prophet Jesaja*, Sechste Auflage, von Dr. Rudolf Kittel, Leipzig, 1898, p. 118.
22. Cyrus H. Gordon: *Belt-Wrestling in The Bible World*, in "Hebrew Union College Annual", Vol. XXIII, Part One, Cincinnati, 1950–1951, pp. 131–6.
23. Illustrations in Gordon: *op. cit.*
24. The text is published in Edward Chiera: *Proceedings In Court.* Publications of the Baghdad School Texts, Vol. IV, Philadelphia, 1934, No. 331.
25. Ivan Engnell: *Studies In Divine Kingship in the Ancient Near East*, Upsala, 1943, p. 133.
26. Young: *Studies In Isaiah*, Grand Rapids, 1954, pp. 166 ff.

Lecture III

THE CONTENT OF OLD TESTAMENT THEOLOGY

OLD Testament theology is concerned with the study of God in His progressive self-revelation in the Old Testament. It has pleased God to make known His truth to mankind by means of a covenant, and the subject-matter with which Old Testament theology is concerned is that covenant which God has made with man for the purpose of man's salvation.

(a) The Meaning of "Covenant"

What, then, is a covenant? And what, in particular, is that covenant which God has made with man? The Hebrew word for covenant is *berît*. It has been assumed that this noun is to be derived from a root meaning *to cut* or *see*. Inasmuch, however, as the word *beritu*, bond, fetter, occurs in Akkadian, it would seem that the Hebrew word is to be connected with this latter. The expressions used in the Old Testament for making a covenant are interesting, the most usual being the idiom, "to cut a covenant" (*kārat berît*). It is interesting to note that this expression has appeared on the Qatna texts, which are probably from the fifteenth century B.C. On these texts the phrase *TAR be-ri-ti* occurs, and may be rendered, "to cut a *beritu*". This expression appears on two tablets, each of which was written by the same man. One tablet contains a list of names, and the other a list of rations. The first list is an agreement or compact in which the men named agree to enter into another's service and to fulfil certain obligations. The rations which are listed on the second tablet are to be received by the men who have bound themselves for the service. In return for their services, the men were to receive specified rations.[1]

As early as the time of the Sumerians there were covenants among the cities and states. These were covenants upheld by an oath and must have gone back to much earlier times. Mendenhall has called our attention to the covenant as developed among the Hittites.[2] Covenants among the Hittites, he says, may be classified as those of suzerainty and those of parity. In the suzerainty covenant the inferior party only is bound by an oath. He must obey the Hittite king because the king demands it. In the parity covenant, however, both of the contracting parties must take the oath and are supposed to abide by it. According to Mendenhall, the suzerainty treaty is the basic form, and he gives as the reason for this the fact that in the parity covenant each party binds the other to identical obligations. As an example he appeals to the treaty between the Egyptian, Ramses II, and the Hittite, Hattusilis. In the suzerainty treaty not only was the vassal to take an oath, but he was also expected to exhibit trust in the king.

In the Hittite and the Babylonian languages the covenant was spoken of by terms such as oaths and bonds, and was regarded as that which was given to the subject by the king or sovereign. "What the description amounts to is this, that the vassal is obligated to perpetual gratitude toward the great king because of the benevolence, consideration, and favour which he has already received. Immediately following this, the devotion of the vassal to the great king is expressed as a logical consequence."[3]

It would be a mistake, however, to proceed from such a survey of the covenant among the Hittites and other peoples and to conclude that a similar form must have appeared also among the Hebrews. Our study of the covenant in the Old Testament must rather be one which is based upon the Old Testament itself. In the course of such a study we may also consider what relationship, if any, exists with the covenants of other ancient nations.

The common expression employed in Hebrew is "to cut a covenant", but other expressions also are employed. We may note the phrases, they "entered into a covenant" (Jer. xxxiv, 10), and "he will cause a covenant to prevail". (Dan. ix, 27) In this latter instance, however, the reference is not to the making of a new covenant, but rather to bringing into force the provisions of a covenant which has already been established.[4] With the common expression for making a covenant, we may note that different prepositions are employed, namely, *l*, *'im* and *bēn*.

In Scripture, the language of the covenants which men are wont to make is employed, but a careful study of the Scriptural phenomena makes it clear that the biblical concept of a covenant is not that of a binding compact or agreement among equals. Nor are conditions necessarily laid down in the making of a covenant. My colleague, Professor John Murray, has defined a divine covenant as "a sovereign administration of grace and of promise. It is not compact or contract or agreement that provides the constitutive or governing idea but that of dispensation in the sense of disposition."[5] If this definition does justice to the Scriptural data, and I believe that it does, we may expect to find the elements of a covenant present, even when there is no express usage of the word itself. Such is, indeed, so.

The covenant, then, which will basically occupy our attention in this study is that in which God promises salvation to man. At this point, however, we find it necessary to differ with many modern treatments of the covenant, which maintain that the covenant was simply that which God made with Israel at Sinai. There was a covenant relationship between Israel and Yahweh, it is claimed, and this covenant relationship was established at Sinai. We are far from denying that a covenant relationship was entered into at Sinai, but what we are now claiming is that that particular manifestation or administration of a covenant at Sinai is not the most fundamental covenant of which the Old Testament speaks. Indeed, a proper understanding of the events of Sinai will make it clear that the covenant of Sinai was only an administration of a covenant which was already in existence.

When the Israelites arrived at Sinai, God identified them as the house of Jacob and the children of Israel. (Exodus xix, 3) The Lord had had previous dealings with them, "Ye have seen what I did unto the Egyptians, and how I bare you on eagles' wings, and brought you unto myself". (Exodus xix, 4) We are reminded of the old Kenite hypothesis, according to which the Israelites adopted Yahweh as their god at Sinai.[6] This adoption was an act of choice upon their part, and, for that reason, so it was maintained, the religion of Yahweh finally developed into an ethical religion. Other views have, in effect, said that there was really no religion of Israel, as such, before Sinai, but merely a worship of the "god of the fathers". It has also been held that before Sinai the religion of the Israelites had passed through various stages of development.

If one considers passages of Scripture which deal with the events at Sinai, however, one cannot escape the conclusion that God had previously dealt with the Israelites by way of covenant. At the burning bush Yahweh identified Himself as "the God of thy father, the God of Abraham, the God of Isaac, and the God of Jacob". (Exodus iii, 6a) Upon hearing this identification, Moses hid his face, and the Scripture states that he feared to look upon God. (Exodus iii, 6b) In other words, Moses recognized that the One Who spoke to him from the midst of the bush was the One Who had made the promises to the patriarchs. Moses was simply to tell the Israelites that the "God of your fathers" (Exodus iii, 13) had sent him unto them. It was this God Who saw what had been done to the Israelites in Egypt and Who had come down to deliver the people. He is furthermore identified as the God of the Hebrews. (Exodus iii, 18) In fact, that which is made clear to Moses at the time of his commission is that the God for Whom he is to approach the people is One Whom the people already know, a God Who has already made promises unto the patriarchs. The Scriptural data, then, make it clear that the first administration of a covenant is not to be found in the events of Sinai.

(b) The Content of The Covenant

The first evidence of the establishment of a covenant with man is found in the second chapter of the Bible, indeed, in the first recorded words of God to man. These words are introduced as a command, and we may render literally, "And the Lord God placed a command upon the man". (Genesis ii, 16) It is to be noticed that the Lord here approaches man and comes before him as the One Who is able to utter commands. Here is no meeting of equals, but the approach of One who is in the position of authority to one who must obey that authority. The words are not a mere request, but a command, spoken with absolute authority.

The command is stated as follows, "Of every tree of the garden thou mayest freely eat: But of the tree of the knowledge of good and evil, thou shalt not eat of it: for in the day that thou eatest thereof thou shalt surely die." (Genesis ii, 16b, 17) It is as the sovereign Authority that God here speaks. The trees of the Garden are His; and man may eat only of those trees which He permits. He grants permission to the man to eat of the trees of the Garden, but from the one tree He withholds this permission. Man has no option; he must obey, for the command has come from the One who alone has the right to utter such a command.

In this passage we learn that God approaches man with a solemn and a sovereign disposition. Man is to obey the command of the Lord, and the outcome, if he obeys, will be for man's blessedness, but if he disobeys, for his ruin. It is true that the command is stated in the form of a prohibition, but, in the light of subsequent events and the remainder of Scripture, we are warranted in saying that, had man obeyed God, he would have passed from a state of probation into one of higher blessedness. What God had done in entering into covenant was something that was intended for man's higher good and blessedness.

It must also be noted that the words of the Lord constitute a gracious warning to man. There is something that Adam must not do; he must not eat of the fruit of a certain tree, for if he does eat, dire consequences will follow. In all of this the Lord appears as One who had Adam's best interests at heart. Indeed, it may be that one reason why the command is stated as a prohibition is to warn man against the tragic consequences which will follow if he disobeys God. It is perhaps more important that man be warned against these consequences than that he be informed of the blessing which would follow obedience. It may be that the reason the blessing is not mentioned is that to have mentioned it would have been to draw the attention of the hearer away from the dreadful consequences of disobedience. Man was left to the freedom of his will, and was in such a state that he might, as he, in fact, did, choose to disobey God. It was for his highest welfare that his attention be directed at this time, not to a future blessedness which would await him if he successfully passed the period of probation, but to the fearful fact of death which would follow disobedience of the commands of God.

It should also be noted that this covenant has to do with the future. It stresses one aspect of the future, namely, the fact that disobedience to the commands of God brings death. Death is something that can come to man, and that must be avoided. What connotation the word "death" may have brought to the mind of the first man is difficult for us to tell. It may be that the word did signify to him that the body would cease its earthly life, but more than that must have been involved. In the Garden Adam had lived in fellowship with God. The Garden belonged to God, and man dwelt in it as a guest. The communion with God which he enjoyed must have been very precious to him. Death would bring about a cessation of that communion.

There is the possibility that God may have spoken more to Adam than is recorded. The account is written for our benefit, and for us it is important to know that the entrance of death into the world was brought about by disobedience on the part of the first Adam. Thus, Adam is placed at the head of human history. Before him lies the future; is it to be a future lived in obedience to the expressly revealed will of God, or is it rather to be a future in which he will act as though God did not exist, in which he will assert that he himself is autonomous?

What if he defies God? What if man becomes a practical atheist, and for all practical purposes denies the existence of God? What if man dies? Those are the questions which in reality occupy the study of Old Testament theology. For that is precisely what happened to man. He disobeyed God, and he died. He fell into sin, and by his act of disobedience he plunged the entire human race also into a state of sin and misery.

What is to be done with this fallen creature, this man who has set himself above God and has fallen into sin and death? According to the Bible, God again approached man. He now approached him, however, as a fallen creature. And the unfolding of the revelation which is given to man as fallen is the content of Old Testament theology. Modern interpretations of the early chapters of Genesis often overlook the fact that God approached man first as an unfallen being, and that He also approached him as a fallen being. God drew near to man in the state of innocency and entered into covenant with him, a covenant which was designed to bring him greater blessing. But He also drew near to man in his fallen state and again entered into covenant, a covenant which was designed to bring to man life and salvation through a Redeemer.

Those views of the early chapters of Genesis which regard them as containing parables, or as relating events which occurred in the spiritual world, or which seek in some form or another to consider them as containing myths have not come to grips with the situation. For none of these views deals in a serious manner with the fact that man was once an unfallen creature, and that, as an unfallen creature, God approached him in covenant. Nor do these views take seriously the fact that man fell into sin. They do not come to grips with the fact that man disobeyed God and so plunged himself, and all mankind descending from him by ordinary generation, into a state of sin and misery. They do not consider, as they should, the fact that God deals with the human race not with individuals but through representatives. There have been, according to the Bible, only two representatives, and these representatives were themselves men. They were the first Adam, the first man, who was of the earth and earthy, but also the second Adam, the second Man, who is the Lord from heaven. If the historicity of the work of Adam is to be discarded, it follows that the analogy which Paul

68

draws between the work of the first Adam and that of the second Adam has no weight.

There is one interpretation only which does justice to the Scriptural data, and that is the one which takes seriously the claims of the Bible that God truly entered into covenant with unfallen Adam, and that He again entered into covenant with fallen Adam. This fact is basic to a proper understanding of all Old Testament revelation. Upon it, indeed, subsequent revelation builds. In fact, the further revelation given in the Old Testament is based upon the presupposition that man is a fallen creature, estranged from God, and that he needs reconciliation to God. The breach which sin has introduced into the relations existing between man and God must be healed, and this work of healing is of God alone.

It is with these thoughts in mind that we consider the approach of God to fallen Adam in the Garden. Again, God draws nigh to man, and again He comes with sovereign power. He asks the questions, and He lays down the conditions. It is necessary that He take the initiative, for man is at enmity with Him and regards Him as his own enemy. When he heard the voice of God in the Garden, Adam hid himself, and his first recorded words were, "I heard thy voice in the garden". (Genesis iii, 10) The hearing of God's voice does not produce joy in his heart. Adam must see that he has transgressed against God. He must confess that transgression, and realize that God is, indeed, his friend, and the serpent his enemy.

Hence, God acts. He announces that He will place enmity between the serpent and the woman. It is interesting to note that He does not command the woman to be at enmity with the serpent. She did not have the power for such enmity. Rather, He Himself must place that enmity between the woman and the serpent, else there can be no enmity. God also announces that this enmity will extend to the respective seeds of the woman and of the serpent, and that it will reach an outcome, in that a decisive capital blow will be struck the serpent, whereas the seed of the woman will receive a lesser blow, being bruised as to the heel.

This protevangelium serves as the basis for the proper understanding of the development of the plan of salvation. At the same time, rightly to understand the protevangelium, one must also note the condition of fallen man, as described in Genesis. In the first place man has now become corrupt. He recognizes that he is naked, and he seeks clothing. Secondly, he has become guilty before God, for upon hearing the voice of the Lord God he seeks to hide himself amidst the trees of the garden. The analysis of sin which is given here is that it first of all involves pollution or corruption of the heart, and that it also involves the sinner in guilt.

It is this picture which forms the necessary background for a correct study of Old Testament theology. But this biblical picture is generally ignored. In his scholarly work, *Die Theologie des Alten Testaments*, Von Rad completely avoids mention of the fact that man is a fallen creature and that a promise of salvation has been made. Instead, the clue to his approach is seen in his sub-title, *Die Theologie der geschichtlichen Überlieferungen Israels*. How does he consider the problem of man's sin? He comes to a study of the Hebrew words *chātā'*, *'awôn* and *pesha'*, and points out that the word *chātā'* refers to all failings of man against God. *'Awôn* is a sin or offence, and contains the concept of consciousness of guilt upon the part of the sinner. *Pesha'* at first belonged to the political, not the cultic sphere, and signified rebellion. Yet it came, especially in the mouth of the prophets, to be the strongest word for sin.[7]

In oldest Israel, maintains Von Rad, sin was every serious violation of the right of God which, in Israel, took the form of a list of cultic prohibitions and general un-written laws.[8] In political life sin was a breaking of the rules of a holy war (Joshua vii); in the family it was the violation of sexual ordinances. (Deut. xxvii, 20 ff.) Sin was an offence against a sacral ordinance. But sin also belonged to a social category. The individual was so closely bound up with the group that, when he com-mitted a sin, it affected the entire community.[9] A further, and important feature, was that the evil deed of the sinner was not to be taken by itself. Rather, when an evil deed had been committed, it set in motion an evil which sooner or later would come back upon the doer thereof or upon the community itself. A most narrow correspondence between the deed and the issue is presupposed; and it is not correct for us to make a distinction or separation be-tween sin and punishment. This is shown, and correctly, we believe, by the fact that the words *chātā'* and *'awôn* do not merely indicate the sin as a separate deed but also include its punishment. "But if ye will not do so, behold, ye have sinned against the LORD: and be sure your sin will find you out." (Numbers xxxii, 23) Von Rad would translate, "your punishment will find you out", and ex-plains this to mean that the deed and its evil consequences will both work back on Israel.[10] The same is seen from the statement of Cain, "My punishment (*'awôn*) is greater than I can bear". (Genesis iv, 13b) It was not merely the evil act, but also the consequences of the act, consequences which would come upon Cain in the form of punishment, that he could not bear. The whole, the evil deed of the murder together with the evil consequences, is summed up in the one word *'awôn*.

It is for this reason, argues Von Rad, that the com-munity was so interested in the sin of the individual. It was not only because sin was a moral matter, an inner disturbing of relations with God, but also because by the sin evil was set in motion which, unless the group acted to break its relation with the individual, would work in a destroying way on the community itself. For this reason, the emphasis must fall on the deed and its objective effect, independent of the consciousness or subjective intention of the sinner himself.

With this picture of Israel's attitude toward sin, one may to a large measure yield formal agreement. At the same time, one cannot rest content with such a picture. Say what one will, it is not a biblical picture, for the Biblical picture presents man as one who is estranged from God by an act of disobedience. Nor does this picture do justice to the fact that sin is an affront against a holy God. Von Rad has made an important point when he indicates that in Scripture the sinful act and its consequences are often regarded as a whole. But it must be noted that the sinner had offended, not so much against the community, as he had against God Himself. "My punishment is greater than I can bear," said Cain, but to whom did he say this? He was in the presence of God Himself, and he realized full well that it was with God that he had to do. On Cain's part there was more concern that he be not hurt by others; his words were through and through selfish. But the punishment that was meted out was a punishment which God had sent, and the banishment of Cain was due to the fact that he had transgressed against God. In the punishment of Cain there is exemplified the truth that "The soul that sinneth, it shall die". (Ezekiel xviii, 20)

Even if we regard the account as nothing more than a story, we may note that the emphasis is nevertheless placed upon a transgression against Yahweh. The act of murder was the result of the fact that the person of Cain and his offering had not been accepted by Yahweh. The punishment was meted out by Yahweh, and even Cain realized that he would be driven out from the face of Yahweh. It was, in other words, a punishment that came upon Cain as an individual. This is not to deny the fact of the solidarity of the race or, even to an extent, of the solidarity of Israel or of the group to which a man belonged. At the same time, first and foremost, sin was a moral transgression against the law of a holy God, and the sinner was punished because of his sin.

This fact is made clear in the legal portions of the Pentateuch. On the day of Atonement, for example, the high priest was to "offer his bullock of the sin offering, which is for himself, and make an atonement for himself, and for his house". (Leviticus xvi, 6) Again, "And Aaron shall bring the bullock of the sin offering, which is for himself, and shall make an atonement for himself, and for his house, and shall kill the bullock of the sin offering which is for himself". (Leviticus xvi, 11) The individual character of sin is also to be seen in such language as "If any man of you bring an offering unto the LORD . . .". (Leviticus i, 2) The individual character of sin cannot be denied. Sin is first and foremost a breach of the law of God upon the part of an individual.

Not only is sin an individual matter, but it is also an offence against God. One has but to read through the book of Leviticus to note how frequently the Lord is mentioned. He is the recipient of the sacrifices. They are offerings which are brought to Him at the altar, and there are presented to Him. They have basically an expiatory character, and terminate primarily not upon the offerer but upon God Himself. We come back, therefore, to the position already adopted, namely, that in the Bible man appears as a fallen creature and that the great theme with which the Old Testament deals is the preparation for the coming of the Redeemer.

The first intimation of the deliverance to come was made to the serpent in the Garden. And if Old Testament theology is to do justice to subsequent material in the Bible, it must certainly do justice to this passage. Dr. Mowinckel writes of Genesis iii, 15, "It is now generally admitted by those who adopt the historical approach to theology that there is no allusion to the Devil or to Christ as 'born of a woman', but that it is quite a general statement of mankind, and serpents, and the struggle between them which continues as long as the earth exists. The poisonous serpent strikes at man's foot whenever he is unfortunate enough to come too near to it; and always and everywhere man tries to crush the serpent's head when he has the chance."[11]

According to Gunkel, the Hebrews asked themselves why the serpent crawled on its belly and did not walk as other animals. The answer is that it was cursed because it deceived mankind. For the narrator of Genesis the serpent is an animal and nothing more, and Gunkel observes that it "does not travel on its belly nor does it eat dust".[12] Furthermore, according to Gunkel, the Hebrews noticed the eternal conflict that went on between mankind and serpents. This conflict would continue as long as there were men and serpents.

Interpretations such as these of Mowinckel and Gunkel must be identified as being based upon a false view of the nature of Scripture. If the Bible is nothing more than a collection of sagas, or if it is simply the "Word" of God or a pointer to the "Word" of God, in some sense consonant with neo-orthodox tenets, it is then impossible to arrive at a correct understanding of its contents. At the same time, it must be acknowledged that neither Mowinckel nor Gunkel has done justice to this text. It should be noted that in the Old Testament the speaking of an animal is very rare. Apart from the speaking of Balaam's ass and the serpent of Genesis iii, animals do not speak. This distinguishes the Old Testament from fable. In the present passage, however, we are not to have recourse to fable because the speaking of the serpent is presented as something most unusual. In Genesis ii the relative position of animals and the man had been established. Adam named the animals, recognizing them as his helpers. They were subject to him. He was distinguished from them in that, among other things, he had an intelligence which enabled him to recognize and to categorize the animals.

In Genesis iii, however, a serpent is presented as speaking. The serpent has left its proper sphere and is placing itself on a par with man. More than that, it is placing itself on a par with God, indeed, even above Him. The language of the serpent is that which leads the woman to an act of transgression against God. The punishment which is inflicted is such as befits a transgression of God's law. Hence, we must conclude that there is something here far deeper than the mere enmity which exists between mankind, on the one hand, and the serpent brood, on the other. It would seem that an evil power had been making the serpent his instrument, through which he communicated with the woman. This time-honoured interpretation of the Church alone does justice to all the phenomena which are presented in Genesis iii. Hence, the deliverance which is to come is not merely that a man will step on the head of a snake. How could that possibly bring about a reversal of the sad condition which obedience to the serpent's words had produced? Rather, a blow was to be struck of such a kind that it would truly bring about a reversal of conditions. This blow would not merely destroy that particular serpent then and there present; it would be far more serious, in that it would destroy him that had used the serpent and that had the power over death itself. The consequence of disobedience was moral. It was spiritual, and the deliverance was to be in keeping therewith; it, too, would be spiritual.

From Genesis iii, 15 it becomes clear that the deliverance of man will be accomplished by an act. It will be an act performed by a seed of the woman. At the same time, it is clear that the working of the Lord in a unique sense is to be seen in this act. The act is prophesied. It is yet in the future, but the Lord predicts its occurrence and also its outcome. It is, therefore, an act which has already been predetermined; and in speaking of it the Lord shows that He truly is the only omniscient One.

Not only, then, does Old Testament theology concern itself with a study of the revelation of God made to man in his unfallen state in the Garden, but it also deals with the unfolding of the plan of salvation to fallen man. And the foundational verse, upon which all subsequent revelation builds, is this protevangelium in Genesis iii, 15. This protevangelium is the first administration of the covenant of grace. At the same time, systematic theology has been true to Scripture in also speaking of a covenant of redemption between the Father and the Son. The very fact that the Lord predicts the outcome of the struggle between the seed of the woman and the seed of the serpent, makes it clear that the outcome was something that had already been determined. In this prediction there is an intimation of the fact that God has already determined upon the salvation of His people.

The covenant of redemption is usually thought of as that covenant made in the councils of eternity between the Father and the Son, wherein the Father promised to the Son an innumerable multitude if the Son would deliver this people from its sin. On the other hand, the covenant of grace is usually identified as the covenant made between God and fallen man. This distinction is perhaps useful, yet we must remember that the two are, in fact, one. When we take into consideration the teaching of the entire Bible, we learn that God had, indeed, determined upon the salvation of His own. In fact, before the foundation of the world they were chosen in Him. The Fall did not come as something unexpected to God. It did not thwart His plans or purposes. Rather, when man had fallen, God appeared in the Garden, bringing His tender and loving overtures of grace, and announcing to fallen man that there was hope and that this hope would be found in One who was to bruise the serpent's head.

When was the Redeemer to come? It apparently seemed to Eve that in the birth of Cain the promise had been fulfilled, for she remarked, "I have acquired a man from the Lord".[13] She looked upon her son as a fulfilment of the promise, and thus at least revealed that she was living a life of faith, based upon the promise made in the Garden. The promised One, however, was not to be a literal son of Eve. Many years were to elapse before His coming. Through these years God was to reveal Himself further to His people. They were to learn much more concerning Him and concerning their own relationship to Him. They were also to learn more of the heinousness of their own sin. God intended to lead His people on by way of preparation until the fullness of the time should come, and then, He would send forth the promised One.

It may now be seen why Messianic prophecy is of such great importance, since Messianic prophecy gives to us the further revelation which serves to identify the Promised One and His work. According to Mowinckel, the figure of the Messiah from the beginning had a political aspect.[14] But in time this political figure took on an eschatological character. We must go back to the kingly ideal of ancient Israel to learn of the origin of the expectations for a future Messiah. Israel took over the model of kingship which was present in Canaan, and, partly because there were in Israel traditions of the old tribal chieftainship, she altered the Canaanite conception of kingship. "The Israelite monarchy", says Mowinckel, "is the result of the fusion of the traditions of the old chieftainship with the laws, customs and ideas of Canaanite kingship".[15] The king in Israel was regarded as a superhuman and divine being; He was Yahweh's anointed, and through this anointing he received superhuman wisdom and power.

The true ideal of kingship, continues Mowinckel, had never actually been fully realized, in Israel, and so the hope arose that some time in the future a truly "Anointed of Yahweh" would come. Thus, the Messiah became an eschatological figure. This very brief sketch, which does not begin to do justice to Mowinckel's views, makes it at least clear that the Messianic hope is regarded as something which later arose in Israel somewhat as a reaction against existing conditions. The biblical picture, however, is precisely the contrary. The Messianic hope, according to the Bible, was not an expectation which simply arose in the course of Israel's history, but, rather, it was a revelation from God given to fallen man for the first time in the Garden of Eden.

(c) Messianic Prophecy

Old Testament theology must devote its attention to a study of the content of the Messianic prophecies. We may, indeed, be grateful for work such as Hengstenberg's *Christology of the Old Testament*, but there is need for similar works which are up-to-date and which take into full account the modern discussions of the passages involved.

At the same time, Messianic prophecy, interesting and useful as it is as a study in itself, must properly be studied in the light of the history of the people of Israel. There is a close relation between the revelations of the Messiah and the historical events in which the nation lived. It is for this reason that we must stress the great epochs in revelation.

We can, perhaps, illustrate this fact by a consideration of the patriarchal age.

Why did not God immediately after the Flood form His people into one great nation and give to them His ordinances? Why did He wait until the events of Sinai before forming His people into a nation? The answer is that it was necessary first to lay the foundations for this nation. The people of God had to be severed from the world. This was done by means of calling Abram from Ur of the Chaldees. At this time, the people of God were few in number. The time had not come for the formation of a nation. There must first be an entrance into the land of promise, and the passing of certain tests. Above all, the people must learn that God would be faithful to the promises which He had made, and that these promises were to be of grace and not of works.

How, therefore, are we to interpret the lives of the patriarchs? Were they simply examples from whose lives we can learn? If they were nothing more than examples, then it would seem to be of no particular import whether they were historical characters or not. It is not to be denied that we may learn from the examples of the patriarchs. They were men of like passions with ourselves, and from their experiences we may profit. At the same time, merely to say that they were examples and nothing more does not do justice to them nor to their position in the history of redemption.

At this point tribute must be paid to the work of the late Dutch scholar, B. Holwerda.[16] Holwerda has pointed out with a unique clarity the fact that the patriarchs are not to be studied merely as examples, but that they were the men upon whom God was founding His Church. Their lives therefore exhibit to us not so much the fact that they at times believed the promises of God, but rather the fact that God Himself was true to the promises which He had made. When the patriarchs are considered in this light, their whole period takes on new meaning.

Thus we read, "For Sarah conceived, and bare Abraham a son in his old age, at the set time of which God had spoken to him". (Genesis xxi, 2) The birth of a child to Abraham makes it clear that the coming salvation is to be entirely of grace and not of works. Abraham and Sarah had to die, as it were, before the child could be born. All reliance upon human strength and power, all confidence in human devices had to be removed. Abraham must be old, and Sarah must be past the time of child-bearing, in order that that which was not possible for man could be seen to be possible for God. When Sarah was as good as dead and so incapable of producing life, then and then alone, was the child of promise born.

The birth of Isaac thus made it clear that the God of the promises was One who could and who would fulfil His promises. It is true that Abraham's faith with respect to this promise had been sorely tried and tested. The first thing that is related of Sarah is that she was barren. (Genesis xi, 30) As though this were not sufficiently emphatic, it is also stated, "she had no child". When Abraham finally enters the land of promise, he, through his own action in Egypt, nearly loses Sarah. After the war with the eastern kings, he cries out in despair, "What wilt thou give me, seeing I go (to the grave) childless?" (Genesis xv, 2) In an attempt to fulfil the promise on his own, Abraham takes Hagar, and Ishmael is born. But Ishmael is not to be the promised seed. Finally, Sarah, long past the age of child-bearing, brings forth Isaac. Abraham is later commanded to sacrifice Isaac. All his life, Abraham was compelled to live in trust, and his faith was sorely tested.

The trial of Abraham's faith, however, is not the great lesson of this portion of Genesis. There is something of greater significance. The obstacles which proved to be tests for Abraham also served to show how great is the saving grace of God. "Sarai was barren; she had no child." (Genesis xi, 30) If the promise of salvation is to be carried out, Sarah, the wife of Abraham, must bear a son. Yet, Sarah is one of whom it would not be expected that she would have a son. And subsequent events seemed to conspire against her having a son. Such was the background against which the grace of God was to be manifested.

In the call of Abraham God was laying the foundation for His Church. He was teaching the patriarch that the promised deliverance could not come as the result of human works or efforts, but was to be a gift of Divine grace alone. For this very reason, it is necessary to insist upon the historicity of the patriarchs. We cannot relegate them to some nebulous realm and speak of a worship of the "god of the fathers", for to do so would be to reject entirely an extremely important epoch of biblical revelation. The unfolding of the covenant of grace has to do with historical events. If the patriarchs are not historical, we do not learn the lesson that the promised salvation was truly to be of grace.

It is in such an historical situation that the Messianic prophecies made to the patriarchs stand out in all their fullness. When Abraham left his fatherland, he was told that in him all the families of the earth would be blessed.[17] It is true that at later stages of the promise this prophecy is couched in the reflexive, but in its first announcement it is correctly translated as a passive. In Abraham others are not merely to bless themselves, but are to be blessed. Abraham is the one through whom God will exhibit the fact that salvation is of grace. He is the one through whom the line of promise will come, and in whom others will also be blessed.

As one traces the Messianic promises which are made in

F

Genesis, one learns that the Messiah is to be a son of Abraham and also that He is to come from Judah. He is to be royal, and he is to bring blessing to the world. The patriarchs walked about the promised land bearing these promises. They truly looked for a city, and so they walked by faith. From the patriarchal period, we have the background against which all the subsequent Old Testament revelation is to be given and against which it is to be understood.

Much scholarship has here gone astray. There has been an emphasis upon the formation of the nation at Sinai, but the roots which connected this nation with the past have not been given sufficient recognition. We are told of Israel's ancestors and forefathers, but in modern discussion little is said about them. The older studies of the history of Israel's religion considered the ancestors of the nation as having passed through various stages of primitive religion. Attempts were made to study various passages of Scripture to detect in them the remnants of this primitive religion. Thus, to give but one example, when Abraham came to the Oak of Moreh at Shechem (Genesis xii, 6), it was thought by some that he came to this spot because there was an oracle or teacher-tree there. In other words, it has been suggested that this particular passage points to a stage in the history of Israel's religion when there was belief in animism. Attempts have been made to trace the progress of belief, from animatism, to animism, to polydemonism, to totemism, and to the final stage of monotheism. This approach brought with it several problems. How, to mention but one, did the tribes come to be united at Sinai? The answer which often has been given is that which has found expression in the so-called Kenite Hypothesis.[18] According to this hypothesis, Yahweh was originally the god of the Kenites among whom Moses dwelt. As Moses shepherded his sheep in the vicinity of Sinai, he pondered the question whether the God of the Mount, Yahweh, the God of the Kenites, could help his own people, the Israelites, who were even then in bondage in Egypt. Apparently, he became convinced that Yahweh could help and that he had commissioned him to go to Egypt and to bring them out. When the people came to Sinai, according to the adherents of this hypothesis, they entered into covenant with Yahweh, and in this very fact, namely, that the religion was one of choice, lay its ethical strength, and the reason why it grew as it did, and why other religions did not so grow.

It must be noted, however, that this explanation does not do justice to the patriarchal period. Were the Israelites simply a nation among the nations? Was there no essential difference between them and other peoples? Is it only the reflection of a much later theology that would say, "For what nation *is there so* great, who *hath* God *so* nigh unto them, as the LORD our God *is* in all *things that* we call upon him *for?*" (Deuteronomy iv, 7) Is that explanation of the uniqueness of Israel entirely to be rejected?

It should be noted that many approaches to the study of the events at Sinai, and, indeed, the more modern approach of regarding the designation "Israel" as applying only after the entrance into Canaan and the establishment of the religious amphyctyony, in reality make a radical break between these events of Sinai or the religious amphyctyony, on the one hand, and the earlier period, on the other. They do not, in fact, speak of a patriarchal period in the traditional Biblical sense. Hence, they are compelled to the conclusion that the wondrous later development of religious expression in Israel was something that arose after the nation had entered the land, or at least, after it had been constituted at Sinai.

Very different, however, is the biblical picture, and the biblical picture makes clear the importance of the patriarchal period. The patriarchs, according to the Bible, were historical characters. They did live in Palestine, and their lives were of the utmost significance for the subsequent development of the people of God. It is, indeed, impossible adequately to account for the later phenomena of religious expression in Israel apart from the patriarchs of Genesis. The foundation for all that follows is to be found in the patriarchal age, with its manifestation of the great truth of salvation by grace and the utterance of the Messianic prophecies, at least in germ form, upon which the remainder of Old Testament history is to be founded.

The biblical picture of the subject-matter of Old Testament theology thus differs radically from that often given today. According to the Bible, the uniqueness of the religion of Israel, if we may use those terms, lay in the fact that Israel possessed God. He dwelt in her midst, and He spoke to her. She was not simply a group of people of unusually fine insight and character, which, through the years, more and more reacted against the circumstances in which she found herself, and gradually came to spiritual and ethical conceptions of God's being and ways. She was rather the recipient of genuine revelation from God.

Old Testament theology is concerned with the study of genuine revelations which the true God gave to Israel. These revelations had to do with His purposes in the salvation of mankind. His plan of salvation may be subsumed under the word covenant. It is, therefore, with the covenant of grace that Old Testament theology is concerned. This is its true content; this is its true subject-matter. In Old Testament theology we study God who has come to man, not man who, on his own initiative, comes, or has come, to God.

It was the purpose of God to bring redemption to man not immediately, but only in the fullness of time. In order to accomplish this, He first formed Israel into a nation. As

84

a preliminary to this formation of the people into a nation, however, there is the patriarchal period, during which the foundation was laid upon which the later theocracy was to be established. For that reason, we have in this lecture paid particular attention to this age of the patriarchs. But the content of Old Testament theology is not to be restricted to this age alone, for it is but preliminary, and Old Testament theology is concerned with each epoch of Biblical revelation.

How grand and ennobling is such a study! We are not dealing with the gropings of ignorant and superstitious Hebrews after God, if haply they might find Him. We are dealing with what God Himself spoke to these Hebrews. They were ignorant; they were in darkness; they were in bondage. But they were the recipients of light. To them the Word of God came, dispelling the darkness, and banishing the ignorance. No longer need they be like the nations round about them, for they were a peculiar people. They could know the truth about God and about their relation to Him, for unto them the very oracles of God had been entrusted.

NOTES TO LECTURE III

1. William F. Albright: *The Hebrew Expression for "Making a Covenant" in Pre-Israelite Documents*, in "Bulletin of the American Schools of Oriental Research", No. 121, Feb. 1951, pp. 21, 22.
2. George E. Mendenhall: *Covenant Forms in Israelite Tradition*, in "The Biblical Archaeologist", Vol. XVII, No. 3, pp. 50–76.
3. This quotation from V. Korosec, *Hethetische Staatsverträge*, Leipzig, 1931, is given by Mendenhall, *op. cit.*, p. 58.
4. Young: *The Prophecy of Daniel*, Grand Rapids, 1949, pp. 191–221.
5. John Murray: *The Covenant of Grace*, London, 1953, p. 31.
6. Karl Budde: *Die Religion des Volkes Israels bis zur Verbannung*, Giessen, 1900.
7. Gerhard Von Rad: *Die Theologie des Alten Testaments*, München, 1957, pp. 261–71.

8. Von Rad. *op. cit.*, p. 262.
9. *Idem*, p. 263.
10. *Idem*, p. 265, Dies Letztere mussten wir mit Strafe übersetzen.
11. Translation by G. W. Anderson in Sigmund Mowinckel, *He That Cometh*, New York, Nashville, p. 11.
12. Hermann Gunkel: *Die Urgeschichte und die Patriarchen* in "Die Schriften des Alten Testaments", Göttingen, 1911, p. 65, "Der Teufel geht nicht auf dem Bauch und frisst keinen Staub."
13. The preposition *'ēṭ* may be rendered "from", like the Akkadian *itti*.
14. *Op. cit.*, pp. 4 ff.
15. *Op. cit.*, p. 59, translation by G. W. Anderson.
16. B. Holwerda: *Dictaten*, Deel 1, *Historia Revelationis Veteris Testamenti*, Kampen, 1954.
17. The verb is here to be translated by the passive. See Oswald T. Allis: *The Blessing of Abraham* in "Princeton Theological Review", Vol. 25, 1927, pp. 263–98.
18. Cf. note 6, *supra*.

Lecture IV

THE INFLUENCE OF OLD TESTAMENT
THEOLOGY

IF Old Testament theology is the study of God in His progressive self-revelation in Old Testament times, it is well to ask what influence, if any, such revelation had. Were the messages which God gave to man, and the mighty acts which He performed on man's behalf, soon to be forgotten, or did they live on and exert an influence in the future development of the plan of salvation? To ask these questions is to answer them.

According to the Bible itself, the period of Old Testament revelation was a period of preparation. It was not an end in itself, but it pointed forward to something that was later to come. This fact may be learned from the Old Testament itself. For one thing, certain promises were made to the patriarchs, and these promises were never fulfilled in Old Testament times. In line with these promises, there is the entire phenomenon of Messianic prophecy. The prophets in their messages exhibited a teleological trend, and the consummation of this trend was never reached during their own lives. The sacrifices also, by their very nature, were preparatory. Such a system of sacrifice could not be continued indefinitely, for it but served to remind the offerer of the great gulf that existed between himself and God, and it never brought to him the assurance that, once and for all times, his sins had been forgiven.

(a) Our Lord's Messianic Consciousness

It will be impossible to trace the influence of Old Testament theology in full detail, and we shall simply note how it has influenced the theology of the New Testament in certain respects. In making our choice we have been guided by certain questions which are much in the forefront of discussion today. First, then, we may note in what respect Old Testament theology has influenced the Messianic consciousness of Jesus Christ.

At the outset it is necessary to enter a caveat. When we discuss the question how in His human nature our Lord came to the consciousness that He was the Messiah prophesied in the Old Testament, we must remember that we are entering a field of great mystery. That Jesus Christ knew that He was the Messiah, there can be no doubt. He is the Eternal Son of God, a Divine Person with a human and a Divine nature, and in His Divine nature, we may say that He knew fully who He was. It is true that in His human nature, there were some things of which He was ignorant, such as the time of the end. (Cf. Matthew xxiv, 36) As a man, He was truly Man, and we may speak of a true growth in His knowledge. Scripture explicitly states that "Jesus increased in wisdom and stature, and in favour with God and man". (Luke ii, 52) If we wish to be true to the Scriptures, we must do full justice to the fact that our Lord was truly a man among men upon this earth.

There is, however, a distinction which must clearly be made. It is one thing to speak of the human nature of the Lord, and of the development of His understanding as a Man. It is one thing to speak of a growth in our Lord's understanding and appreciation of His Messianic consciousness. It would, however, be a gross misunderstanding of Scripture to assert that our Lord only became the Messiah as He understood His vocation. He was the Messiah, the Son of David, the Anointed One, who had come to this earth for the specific purpose of saving His people from their sins by the shedding of His most holy and precious blood. On that point, there can be no doubt whatsoever. The Scripture is explicit. "He shall be great, and shall be called the Son of the Highest: and the Lord God shall give unto him the throne of his father David: And he shall reign over the house of Jacob for ever; and of his kingdom there shall be no end." (Luke i, 32, 33) The fact that He was the Messiah, and the problem of His understanding in His human nature of His Messianic task are two different subjects, and they must never be confused. It can only result in great misunderstanding if these two problems are confused, and it is likely also to result in a depreciation of the true identity of our Lord. He was the Messiah, the One who should come, the One of whom the prophets prophesied. At the same time, in His own human nature there was a growth in His understanding of what was involved in His Messianic office and work.

It has been necessary to state these features with some care, in order that it may be made clear that we believe that Jesus Christ is the true Messiah. We wish to repudiate any views which would identify His becoming the Messiah or entering upon the rôle of Messiah with His own understanding of that office, or which would in any sense minimize the fact that He is truly a Divine Person, the omniscient Son of God.

Our purpose at the present is rather to examine in brief fashion what the Messianic consciousness was which our Lord held. How did Jesus Christ conceive His office of Messiah, and in what way was that position in accord with what the Old Testament had to say on the subject? The traditional answer to this question is that Jesus Christ was the Prophet, Priest and King, and that it was as such that the Messianic prophecies depicted Him. Such a designation is accurate and true to the Scriptures. It is fundamental and we shall probably never improve on it. At the same time, it is not so detailed as it might be. In recent times, Geerhardus Vos has analysed the self-consciousness of our Lord, and has sought to discover what were the essential elements in that consciousness.[1] It is important that the word "essential" be emphasized. The essential elements are those without which there could be no concept of Messiahship. In the Old Testament it was prophesied, for example, that the Messiah would be born in Bethlehem. The place of birth, however, is hardly an essential element in the Messianic picture. Conceivably, our Lord could have been born elsewhere. The precise place of His birth was not an essential element in His mission.

Vos finds five elements in the consciousness of Messiahship as held by Jesus Christ, which he regards as essential. The first of these he designates the regal element. Stated simply, this means that the Messiah was to be a king who would reign with absolute authority. The manner in which our Lord, to give but one example, sets Himself over against what had been said in former times, when He declares "For I say unto you", is clear evidence that He believed Himself to be One Who possessed complete authority. He speaks in the Sermon on the Mount with independent authority. He is not relying upon what the rabbis and Jewish teachers have said, but upon His own authority, and the commands which He utters are those which must be obeyed. (Cf. Matthew v, 20–43)

Secondly, the eschatological element is prominent in our Lord's Messianic consciousness. This element is seen in the passage to which appeal has just been made, the Sermon on the Mount. In this passage the Lord sets Himself forth as over against what had preceded. He is, as it were, the last word. As Vos says, "Jesus being consciously the Messiah, his whole manner of thinking and feeling could not be otherwise than steeped in this atmosphere.

It was an atmosphere in which the currents of air from this world and from the world to come constantly intermingled, with the stronger breeze steadily blowing toward the future."[2]

Thirdly, there is the element of supernaturalism. The coming of the Messiah revealed the coming of God. His entrance into the world was a manifestation of the supernatural working of God. This is seen, for example, in the mighty miracles which our Lord performed. He came into this world, one might say, on a wave of the supernatural.

Fourthly, Vos mentions the soteriological aspect of the Messianic consciousness. This element consists in the fact that our Lord believed Himself to be the Saviour. He came for the purpose of saving His people from their sins. "For even the Son of man come not to be ministered unto, but to minister, and to give his life a ransom for many." (Mark x, 45) Vos stresses this element to such an extent that he says, "Without the hope of salvation to be wrought through Him the greater part of the Messiah's reason of existence would fall away".[3] Such emphasis is not overdrawn. Jesus Christ is the Saviour, and it is as such that His people delight to speak of Him.

Lastly, there is the fact that the Messiah is not to be merely a man, not even the greatest and best of men, but rather is to be God Himself. He is to be a Divine person, not in the modern sense in which the word "Divine" is robbed of its meaning, but in the fullest sense of the word, so that we may say that He is as to deity one with the Father. He identified Himself explicitly with the Father when He remarked, "I and my father are one". (John x, 30) We may note also His strange language in the closing verses of the eleventh chapter of Matthew, "All things are delivered unto me of my Father: and no man knoweth the Son, but the Father; neither knoweth any man the Father, save the Son, and *he* to whomsoever the Son will reveal *him.* Come unto me, all ye that labour and are heavy laden, and I will give you rest. Take my yoke upon you, and learn of me; for I am meek and lowly in heart: and ye shall find rest unto your souls. For my yoke *is* easy, and my burden is light." (Matthew xi, 27–30) Without seeking to multiply evidence further, we may simply appeal to our Lord's usage of the term "Son of Man", for in this appeal alone there is clear proof that Jesus Christ believed Himself to be God in the fullest sense.[4]

What is the relationship which this consciousness sustains to the theology of the Old Testament? If one were to say that our Lord simply allowed the Old Testament to influence Him as to what He should believe, justice would not be done to the facts. Jesus Christ did not simply find in the Old Testament some thought which helped Him to form His own Messianic consciousness. Such a view does not do justice to the phenomena of Scripture. The concept of Messiahship which our Lord held was one which had been predicted in the Old Testament. Jesus was the Messiah because He fulfilled what had been spoken concerning Him in the Old Testament. He was the very One of whom the prophets spake. He came into this world for the explicit purpose of fulfilling what they had written concerning Him. Therefore, as He increased in wisdom and stature, we may be assured that His own conception of Messiahship was precisely that which the Old Testament had pictured.

This conception of Messiahship is, indeed, the same as is found in the Old Testament. It is impossible to discover each of these elements in every one of the Messianic prophecies, but they are all found in the total picture of the Messiah which the Old Testament gives. From this point of view, then, we may analyse the first of the Messianic prophecies, a prophecy that was uttered by the Lord Himself. The first feature which strikes the reader is the fact of the Divine working. It is God Himself who is to establish the enmity between the serpent and the woman. The note of the supernatural is thus seen to be present at the very beginning of redemptive history. To the believer of Old Testament times, salvation was to be connected with the work of the Lord. In it there would be manifested a true supernaturalism. We note also that the enmity which was to exist between the serpent and the woman would extend to their respective seeds and would culminate in a decisive blow, wrought by the seed of the woman. Here is the eschatological element. It is true that this element appears in this particular prophecy in germ form, but it does appear. There will be an enmity which will be continuous. At the same time, it will not be an everlasting enmity, but will come to an end, and it will come to an end in that the seed of the woman will strike a blow which will bruise the serpent as to the head. Beyond this, there will be no need for any further blow to be struck.

In this prophecy we may also discern the element of soteriology. The promise is evidently uttered for the benefit of the man and the woman who had hid themselves from before the presence of the Lord in the midst of the trees of the Garden. They had feared to face God, for they were conscious that they were guilty before Him and so were liable to His condemnation and punishment. The Lord, however, did not immediately drive them from the Garden, but rather pronounced upon the serpent a curse, and made the announcement of deliverance. The statement that the seed of the woman would deliver a fatal blow was an announcement of hope. For one thing, it made clear that the woman would have a seed. She would not immediately die, but would produce an offspring which would defeat the serpent. This was the understanding which Adam and Eve had of the prophecy, for they evidently believed it to be true. Adam names his wife

93

Eve, *chawwāh*, a word which signifies that she would, indeed, be the source of life.[5] By this act he showed that he believed that the prophecy would be fulfilled. At the birth of Cain, Eve declared that she had received a man child from the Lord, evidently thinking that in Cain the promise was to be realized. She was mistaken, but, at least, her words make it clear that she did believe that there would be a decisive blow struck which would right the condition of things that sin had introduced. In this first of all Messianic prophecies, therefore, we may note the elements of supernaturalism, eschatology and soteriology.

It is not long, however, before the other elements also make their appearance. In the prophecy uttered by Noah, the regal element is also present. In this prophecy, for the first time in Scripture, the Lord is identified as the God of a particular people. "Blessed be the Lord God of Shem." (Genesis ix, 26) Canaan is said to become the servant of Shem, and Japheth is also to dwell in the tents of Shem. There is difficulty in the interpretation of this prophecy, for, as the language stands, it is ambiguous. The ambiguity appears particularly in verse 27, which reads, "God shall enlarge Japheth, and he shall dwell in the tents of Shem. . . ." It is not clear from the language itself who is to dwell in the tents of Shem, whether it be Japheth or God. Nor is it clear in what sense this dwelling, if it is to be that of Japheth, is to take place. If Japheth is the one who is to dwell in the tents of Shem, is it to be the forced dwelling of a conquered people, or is it to be that of a sojourner or of a guest? The answer to these questions can be determined only by the fulfilment of the prophecy. Subsequent prophecy shows that Japheth is to dwell in the tents of Shem, and that the fulfilment of the prophecy took place with the inclusion of the Gentile nations in the kingdom of God. The submission upon the part of Japheth, therefore, is to be made to Shem, for Shem is to receive the blessing of being the nation whose God is the Lord. Thus, although again in germ form and presented in a mysterious fashion, the regal element, or that of absolute authority, appears in the prophecy.

When we come to the series of promises granted unto Abraham, we find that the same elements appear in one form or another. The complete supernaturalism of the promises is not only mentioned but is prominent. This fact is seen in the first of these promises. In the language of Genesis xii, 1–3, the Lord appears as the One who has the sovereign disposal of all things in His own hands. The land is one which He will show to Abraham, and the destinies of those who come into contact with Abraham are in His hands. Those who bless Abraham, He will bless, and those who curse him, He will curse. The element of soteriology is also apparent in the announcement that in Abraham all the families of the earth will be blessed.

The regal element comes to particular promise in the words spoken in Genesis xvii, "kings of people shall be of her". (Genesis xvii, 16) The same element is found in Genesis xlix, 10, in the famous Shiloh prophecy, and appears again in the words of Balaam, "I shall see him, but not now; I shall behold him, but not nigh: there shall come a Star out of Jacob, and a Sceptre shall rise out of Israel, and shall smite the corners of Moab, and destroy all the children of Sheth." (Numbers xxiv, 17) It is in 2 Samuel vii that this regal element comes to explicit prominence. Upon this chapter are founded the regal Psalms and the many promises of the later prophecies, which have to do with the reign of the Messianic king.

How clearly the regal element appears, for example, in the words of Isaiah, "For unto us a child is born, unto us a son is given: and the government shall be upon his shoulder: and his name shall be called Wonderful Counsellor, The mighty God, The everlasting Father, The

Prince of Peace. Of the increase of *his* government and peace *there shall be* no end, upon the throne of David, and upon his kingdom, to order it, and to establish it with judgment and with justice, from henceforth even for ever. The zeal of the LORD of hosts will perform this." (Isaiah ix, 6, 7) If anything is clear from the Old Testament, it is that the coming Messiah is to be a king. In this respect, the harmony between the Old Testament prophecy and Our Lord's Messianic consciousness is complete.

The same is true with respect to the element of supernaturalism. The verses to which reference has just been made teach that the birth and the reign of the Messiah will be wrought by the zeal of the Lord of hosts. The salvation which the Messiah is to accomplish is also said to be the work of the Lord. "It pleased the LORD to bruise him; he hath put *him* to grief." (Isaiah liii, 10a) In order to accomplish His purpose, God performed mighty miracles in Old Testament times. He displayed His power at the time of the Exodus, at the period when the true religion was threatened by the Tyrian Baal worship which Jezebel had introduced, and during the period of the Babylonian captivity. Surely, the element of supernaturalism is prominent throughout the promises of the Old Testament which have to do with the Messiah.

The Old Testament prophecies likewise have much to say about eschatology. "In that day", says Amos, "will I raise up the tabernacle of David that is fallen, and close up the breaches thereof; and I will raise up his ruins, and I will build it as in the days of old. . . ." (Amos ix, 11) Daniel, before interpreting the vision which had to do with the Messianic kingdom, said to the king, "But there is a God in heaven that revealeth secrets, and maketh known to the king Nebuchadnezzar what shall be in the latter days." (Daniel ii, 28a) And we may note Isaiah's description of the Messianic kingdom, "And it shall come to pass in the last days, that the mountain of the LORD's house shall be established in the top of the mountains, and shall be exalted above the hills; and all nations shall flow unto it." (Isaiah ii, 2) Throughout all the prophecies, there is a definite teleological trend, a pointing forward to an age to come, an age when the Messiah will appear upon the earth, the eschatological age. It is the fullness of the times, the culmination of history, the last days.

It goes without saying that the soteric element is prominent in the Old Testament. One need but consider the Levitical sacrifices and Isaiah liii. In this latter passage, in particular, one has as clear a picture of the saving work of the Messiah as can be found even in the New Testament. In this prophecy the salvation depicted is to be spiritual. It is the removal of sin which is in view and this is to be accomplished by the Servant of the Lord, in that He bears the iniquities of the guilty. He bears their iniquities, and they, in return, receive His righteousness. Here is the Gospel, and it cannot be removed from this passage. That the work of salvation is spiritual is also to be seen from the fact that salvation is always connected with the coming and the work of God Himself. It is that which He alone accomplishes.

Is the Messiah conceived as divine in the Old Testament? Despite the many voices that are raised to the contrary and the desperate efforts of George Adam Smith to maintain that in Isaiah ix, 6 the Messiah is not called God in a metaphysical sense, it must be asserted that that particular passage does attribute Deity to the Messiah. For one thing, it employs the word *pele'* of the child that is born, and this word serves as a designation of Deity. In the second place the word *'el*, which is employed of the Messiah, is clearly used in Isaiah of God. What Isaiah is saying is that the Messiah is an *'el* of a *gibbôr*, a god of a mighty one, that is, He is a mighty One who is God.[6]

The Deity of the Messiah also appears in that majestically-conceived vision of the Son of Man in Daniel vii. The Son of Man is a heavenly being to whom the peoples of the earth bring service. He comes with the clouds of heaven in glory to perform the work of judgment, a work which belongs to God alone. In Micah v, 2 also we have an indication of the Deity of the Messiah. In addressing Bethlehem, the prophet says, "But thou, Bethlehem Ephratah, *though* thou be little among the thousands of Judah, yet out of thee shall he come forth unto me *that is* to be ruler in Israel; whose goings forth *have been* from of old, from everlasting." (Micah v, 2) The Messiah of the Old Testament, then, is one who is Deity Himself. It may be that the prophets did not fully understand those things of which they spoke. They uttered in seed form truths which would be completely revealed only in the New Testament age, but they did point forward to that One who was to come, and the words which they spoke have found their true explanation and fulfilment in Him.

We may thus note that in this particular sphere the theology of the Old Testament has prepared the way for the coming of the Messiah. He, indeed, was the One of whom the prophets spoke, and the picture which they gave of Him was one that fitted in precisely with what He Himself understood of His own Person and the nature of His own work.

(b) The Messiah's Saving Work

A second place where we may note the influence of the Old Testament teaching has to do with the saving work of the Messiah, in particular. If there is anything that is clear from the New Testament, it is that the picture of Jesus' saving work which the New Testament offers is one that is in complete harmony with that offered by the Old Testament. At the very pinnacle of Old Testament prophecy stands Isaiah liii. The One of Whom this chapter speaks is designated the Servant of the Lord. In this chapter, the Servant is depicted as suffering vicariously in the place of others and for their sins. There can be little doubt but that this is the teaching of the chapter. "He was wounded for our transgressions, he was bruised for our iniquities: the chastisement which procured our peace was upon him, and with his stripes we are healed. (Isaiah liii, 5—author's translation) It is precisely this same conception of the saving work of the Servant which is also found in the New Testament. It is found first of all in our Lord's own words, when He says that even "the Son of Man came not to be ministered unto, but to minister, and to give his life a ransom for many". It is found in the words of the administration of the Last Supper when Christ said, "For this is my blood of the new testament, which is shed for many for the remission of sins." (Matthew xxvi, 28)

It is in the epistles of Paul that the Old Testament conception of vicarious suffering is made very prominent. "I am crucified with Christ: nevertheless I live; yet not I, but Christ liveth in me: and the life which I now live in the flesh, I live by the faith of the Son of God, who loved me, and gave himself for me." (Galatians ii, 20) And again, "For he hath made him to be sin for us, who knew no sin; that we might be made the righteousness of God in him." (2 Corinthians v, 21) Or we may note, "Whom God hath set forth to be a propitiation through faith in his blood, to declare his righteousness for the remission of sins that are past, through the forbearance of God: To declare, I say, at this time, his righteousness: that he might be just, and the justifier of him which believeth in Jesus." (Romans iii, 25, 26) The picture of the work of salvation which we find in the New Testament is the same as that which had previously been revealed in the Old.

(c) The Apostolic Missionary Preaching

It is with respect to the missionary preaching of the early Church that we may also note the influence of the teaching of the Old Testament. As a sample of Paul's missionary preaching, it may be apposite to quote his words to the Thessalonians, "For they themselves shew of us what manner of entering in we had unto you, and how ye turned to God from idols, to serve the living and true God; And to wait for his Son from heaven, whom he raised from the dead, even Jesus, which delivered us from the wrath to come." (1 Thessalonians i, 9–10)

This passage, which contains the heart of the missionary preaching in which the apostle Paul engaged, stands forth almost as a compendium of Old Testament theology. In the first place, the Old Testament makes it prominent that the Gentiles were to receive the grace of God in salvation. This had been suggested as early as Noah's prophecy, for Japheth was to dwell in the tents of Shem. It received greater stress in the words of Jacob concerning Shiloh, "The sceptre shall not depart from Judah, nor a lawgiver from between his feet, until Shiloh come; and unto him *shall* the gathering of the people *be*." (Genesis xlix, 10) The peoples, the *'ammîm*, are they who are apart from Shiloh, but who, when he comes, are to be gathered unto him. This thought is found throughout the Old Testament and lays the basis for the missionary preaching of the Gospel by the early apostolic Church. The thought appears, for example, in the message of Isaiah, "And in that day there shall be a root of Jesse, which shall stand for an ensign of the people; to it shall the Gentiles seek: and his rest shall be glorious." (Isaiah xi, 10)

It is necessary to stress this universalistic emphasis of the Old Testament. Sometimes, the charge is made that the Old Testament presents merely a narrow, nationalistic, selfish type of religion. One can only assume that such a charge is due to an ignorance of the true teaching and emphasis of the Old Testament. The nation of Israel was chosen by God to be a light to the Gentiles, to be the centre from which the true religion was to shine forth to the entire world. This was the Divine intention, but Israel rebelled against God and showed herself to be a nation stiff of neck and hard of heart. The true picture of Israel is well given in the first message of Isaiah, "I have nourished and brought up children, and they have rebelled against me." (Isaiah i, 2b) It is strange that anyone should suggest that Israel had a genius for religion, for, according to the Bible, that for which Israel had a genius was rebellion and apostasy.

The nations should have been blessed through Israel. Instead, however, the nations finally were used of God to remove Israel from her land. The Chaldeans were employed by God as His tool or instrument for the purpose of taking away the chosen people from its inheritance. Although they themselves believed that they were acting in their own power and strength, nevertheless, they were, in fact, under the control of the sovereign God, and were carrying out His purposes. It was not through the physical, historical nation of Israel that the earth at that time was to receive its blessing. At the same time, sinful as was this nation, it was the chosen nation, and through it there did come in the fullness of time the One who was to redeem His own people from every nation, tongue and kindred upon the face of the earth. The missionary preaching of the apostles, therefore, was in line with the preparation which the Old Testament had made.

Nor did the content of such preaching differ essentially from what had been taught in the Old Testament. "Ye turned to God from idols," says the Apostle in his message to the Thessalonians. Herein is set forth the necessity of conversion, not only a turning away from falsehood and sin but a turning unto the true God. The Old Testament had provided a remarkable background for this preaching in its strong condemnation of idolatry. "They that make a graven image *are* all of them vanity; and their delectable things shall not profit; and they *are* their own witnesses; they see not, nor know; that they may be ashamed." (Isaiah xliv, 9) It will not be necessary to multiply verses to prove this, for in this one brief verse Isaiah has summed up as it were what the Old Testament has to say about idols and idolaters. The people of God in olden times were not to take part in idolatry, and this very emphasis appears in the preaching of the apostles. If the true faith is to be embraced, there must be a renunciation of all idolatry.

The next feature which the Apostle stresses is that the Thessalonians turned from idols, in order that they might serve the living God. The conversion which the Apostle proclaimed was a real conversion. There must not only be a complete break with the past, a complete break with idolatrous worship, but there must also be a positive serving of the living and true God. Again, the Apostle is in perfect harmony with the Old Testament emphasis. If there is any one thought that is made prominent in the Old Testament, it is that God is the true God; in contradistinction to the dead idols, He is the living God. He possesses an objective metaphysical existence, independent of man. He is sovereignly above His creation. If we begin with the first verse of the Bible, we may find this truth taught through the Old Testament. It also forms the basis of the Apostle's message. Indeed, it is not too much to say that the greatest need of the present day is for a return to this emphasis. There is a great danger that in the study of the Bible and even in the preaching of the Gospel, our thoughts and activities will not be God-centred. There is the danger that the entire emphasis will be placed on man, and that we shall neglect or even deny God. In the Old Testament there is a clear-cut, robust theism, and this same clear-cut, robust theism underlies the missionary preaching of the apostles.

Paul next mentions the Second Coming. Here again, he is building on what has been revealed in the Old Testament. It is true that the Old Testament does not identify the Second Coming of the Lord in precisely those words, but it does point out that there will come an end to the present order and particularly to the work of antichrist.[7] What Paul here asserts is based upon Old Testament teaching; it is, indeed, a development of such teaching; it is a further revelation given by the Spirit of God, no doubt, but it is consonant with what had already been revealed in the Old Testament.

Paul then stresses the saving work of Jesus Christ, which also is in line with what had previously been revealed in the Old Testament. The atonement and the resurrection fit in beautifully with what the Old Testament had taught. In Isaiah liii, to give an example, the atonement is clearly set forth, and also the fact that the servant after death lives again. Here, at least, is a preparation for the later-to-be-revealed truth of the resurrection. Lastly, Paul speaks of the wrath to come. For this doctrine, also, there had been preparation. The Old Testament clearly teaches that death is a punishment for sin. And the death of which the Old Testament speaks would often seem to involve more than the mere cessation of physical life. There is also present at times the thought of alienation from God and His blessings. Such a phrase as "to be cut off from the congregation of Israel" may refer to death, but there is also implicit in it the thought of a being severed from all the blessings which the congregation of Israel may bring to a person. The principle of punishment for transgression is present in the Old Testament, as well as the fact of the intrusion at times of the wrath of God. Hence, what Paul asserts with respect to that from which Jesus Christ had saved the Thessalonians was something that had its roots in the teaching of the Old Testament.

(d) The Church's Official Teaching

There is one other feature on which we may note the influence of Old Testament theology. It is in the official teaching of the Church of Christ. We make reference now not to the apostolic Church but to the Christian Church in its later development. From time to time that Church has felt herself compelled to make official pronouncements in the form of creeds as to her belief. Has the Church in so doing been biblical or has she not? Do her creeds reflect the teaching of the Bible or do they not? One of the greatest of her creeds is that of the Council of Chalcedon, A.D. 451, in which the Church made some very definite statements about the Person of Jesus Christ. Of our Lord it said that He was "truly God and truly Man of a reasonable soul and body, of one essence (homoousion) with the Father according to the Godhood and one nature with us according to the Manhood".[8]

In these words of the Council there was set forth the universal faith of the Church. In commenting upon the two natures in the Person of our Lord, Charles Hodge says, "Christ's person is theoanthropic, but not his nature; for that would make the finite infinite, and the infinite finite. Christ would be neither God nor man; but the Scriptures constantly declare Him to be both God and man. In all Christian creeds, therefore, it is declared that the two natures in Christ retain each its own properties and attributes. They all teach that the natures are not confounded . . ."[9]

In recent days this fundamental doctrine of the Christian faith has come under severe attack, by those who think that some form of irrationalism and dialecticism should supplant the historic faith. One of the most telling blows against the historic Christian and Scriptural doctrine has been made by Karl Barth who thinks that this historic creed of the Church stands in need of re-interpretation. We must avoid making a static separation between the divine and the human natures of Christ, thinks Barth.[10] Charles Hodge has said, "If divine attributes be transferred to man, he ceases to be man; and if human attributes be transferred to God, he ceases to be God. The Scriptures teach that the human nature of Christ remained in its integrity after the incarnation; and that the divine nature remained divine."[11] This, however, according to Barth, is to maintain a static separation between the human and the Divine natures of Christ.

It soon becomes apparent that Barth is widely separated in his thinking on this not only from the position of the historic Christian Church, but what is of infinitely greater importance, from the Bible itself. Christ is what He does, says Barth, and what He does He always has done. He insists that the humanity of Christ is inherently integral with the Divinity.[12] The old orthodox Christology suffered, thinks Barth, from the pride of man who makes God in his own image.[13] It is difficult to understand how a Christian man can speak as Barth here does, for he has made a vigorous attack upon the historic Christian faith. The dialecticism which characterizes Barth's attack upon the doctrine of the Person of Christ is based upon a philosophical position which is in its very nature hostile to that supernaturally-revealed religion known as Christianity. It is not our purpose, nor should we be able at the present time to investigate more thoroughly that philosophical background.[14] But we may surely affirm without fear of successful contradiction that Barth's position, whatever else may be said about it, is not biblical, while that of the Council of Chalcedon is biblical.

In the pronouncement of the Council of Chalcedon we see the historic Church engaged in the all-important and significant task of formulating her doctrine. At the same time, she was also bearing a witness to the entire world, proclaiming to that world the truth concerning the Redeemer whom she loved and in whose precious blood she trusted for salvation. It should be noted that the work of doctrinal formulation is at the same time also a missionary endeavour; it is the proclamation of the truth. In the carrying out of such a task the Council of Chalcedon did not formulate a doctrine of what she, relying upon mere human wisdom, thought she should assert about Christ. Rather than that, she turned to the Scriptures, and the pronouncements which she made were those that were based upon, and formulated in accordance with, what the Scriptures taught. If Barth's cry for a re-interpretation of Chalcedon were based on a desire to consider that Council's pronouncements in the light of genuine Biblical exegesis, there could be no reasonable criticism. A Christian and a Church should always examine their creeds in the light of the Bible. The Bible is the revelation of God, not the creeds. The Bible never needs revision, but as the Holy Spirit illumines His Church, there is need for more and more careful study of our formulations of the faith. It is true that as we progress in an understanding of the Scriptures our creeds may need revision. Barth's approach, however, is different. It is one which is really at variance with what the Bible teaches.

How may Old Testament theology be of help at this stage? It may be of help in that it supports the position of the New Testament with respect to the Person of our Lord. It may be of help in that it shows how the Church in her proclamation and formulation of doctrine has been influenced by the Bible. Here is one feature in which the influence of Old Testament theology may clearly be discerned.

What, then, does the Old Testament have to say about the Person of the Redeemer? In answer to this question it must be remembered that the Old Testament does not present the same full revelation of saving truth that is later found in the New. The Old is preparatory, and its revelation is also preparatory. That does not mean that the revelation which is found therein is not true and genuine. It is true, and it is genuine. It does not require abrogation by later revelations as is so with supposed revelations in the Koran. The material which the New Testament develops is found in the Old Testament and this is true also of the doctrine of the Person of our Lord. It may, then, be said with confidence that the formulation of the doctrine which was made at Chalcedon is one that is consonant with the revelation of the Old Testament. Indeed, the foundation of that doctrine is found in the Old Testament.

First, it should be noted that in the Old Testament the distinction between God and man is always made very clear. There is no admixture of the divine and the human, such as is common in some of the religions of antiquity. At the very beginning of the Bible we read, "In the beginning God created the heaven and the earth". (Genesis i, 1) A proper exegesis of this verse, we believe, makes clear that the verse does teach an absolute creation, as *creatio ex nihilo*. Throughout the first chapter of Genesis God is presented as supreme above His creation. He speaks and His will is carried out. The scheme of fiat and fulfilment shows that He is truly sovereign.

The distinction between God and man which is set forth in Genesis i is maintained with absolute consistency throughout the Old Testament. The distinction is never broken down, so that God is identified with man or man with God. "I am God and not man; the Holy One in the midst of thee." (Hosea xi, 9b) These words well sum up the teaching of the Old Testament with respect to the separation which exists between God and man.

Nor is this distinction in any sense broken down or modified in those portions of the Old Testament in which there are adumbrations of the doctrine of the Trinity. Thus, the Angel who met Hagar in the wilderness, although he is identified as the Lord, and although Hagar herself identified Him as "Thou God seest me", and although He spoke as only God can speak, nevertheless, He maintains the distinction between Himself and man. "I will multiply thy seed exceedingly, that it shall not be numbered for multitude." (Genesis xvi, 10) It is the Angel who performs the wondrous work of multiplication. He does not in any sense, however, identify Himself with the seed itself.

What, however, are we to say about a Messianic prophecy, such as Isaiah ix, 5, 6, in which mention is made both of the Divine and the human nature of the Messiah? That the reality of the human nature is present there can be no doubt. "For a child, he is born to us, a son, he is given to us."[15] Thus, it is plainly taught that the child appeared upon this earth by way of birth; he is a true human. At the same time, the names which are conferred upon the Child show that he was something more than human. He is a wonder of a counsellor, and this designation shows that He is truly God. The word *pele'* was used of the Angel who appeared unto Manoah and his wife. The root is used of the wonders which God performed in Egypt. In thus identifying the child as a *pele'*, the prophet is designating Him as a truly Divine Person.

Here, then, in one verse we are taught the humanity of the Child and also His Deity. Are the two, however, confused? Does the divine flow into the human, or is the human taken up into the divine? Is there anything in this verse which would support the erroneous view of Barth that Christ's humanity is inherently integral with His Divinity? It should be noted that the language of this Old Testament passage is remarkably restrained. There is mystery here. The verse does not tell us all that we might desire to know. And the difficulty is heightened by the statement that "the Lord of hosts will perform this". (vs 7b) A truly human child is to be born, that much is clear. He is to perform the functions of a ruler, in that the government is to be upon His shoulder. He is also the Prince of Peace, which is a fitting designation for a human ruler. At the same time, the predicates of Divinity also are made of Him. In one breath, as it were, the prophet identifies Him as human and as divine. He is God and He is Man.

A superficial view of this passage would claim that the strong distinction between God and Man which the Old Testament makes everywhere else is here broken down. Such, however, is not so. It is true that the prophet speaks of one Individual as Man and also as God, but the prophet, in so speaking, does not break down the distinction between the two which is found throughout the Old Testament. The two appear in the one Individual, but the two are not confused. What Isaiah says of the Child may truly be spoken of a human being; what he says of the Child may truly be spoken of God. The divine is not minimized or lessened in order that the human may be more elevated or exalted; nor is the human stressed in such a way as to obscure the divine. The divine does not take up the human into itself, nor does the human partake of the divine to raise itself. The one does not flow into the other, nor are the two in any sense mingled together, nor fused into one. The divine is truly present, and the human is truly present, but they are not in such a way that the divine is not really divine nor the human really human. In speaking of our Lord Jesus Christ as it did, the Council at Chalcedon spoke in perfect accordance with the teaching of the Old Testament. It brought out in its utterance the truth which lay in germ form in the ninth chapter of Isaiah's prophecy.

On the other hand, the criticism which Barth and others have levelled against the formulations of Chalcedon are criticisms that cannot be supported from the Scriptures. They are criticisms which are not biblical. They are not true to the biblical way of thinking, and they seek to impose upon the Bible a way of thinking quite foreign to it. The Council of Chalcedon, we may safely say, was thoroughly biblical in the formulation of the doctrine which it produced. Indeed, Old Testament theology definitely did influence the Church in her statement of the truth.

In this connection, Old Testament theology serves as a useful handmaid to the discipline of Systematic Theology. There has appeared a tendency to depreciate Systematic Theology at the expense of what some would call biblical theology. Systematic Theology, however, is simply the formal statement of the teaching of the Bible. Can there be anything more important than to know what the Bible has to say about God, about man's relation to God, and the duty which God requires of man? It is here that Old Testament theology has wrought its blessed influence, for the formulations of truth made by theologians and by the Councils of the Church have been in line with the teaching of the Old Testament itself.

(e) Conclusion

How important and significant is this study of Old Testament theology! It is of particular importance in the present day when there is a substitute claiming the throne, a substitute which also goes by the name of Old

Testament theology. The two, however, can easily be distinguished. Just as one who desires to detect counterfeit money will do well to study the genuine, so that he knows it thoroughly, so also can one who knows true Old Testament theology easily detect that which is false. The one is truly theology, for it studies the revelation of God; the other is not theology, for it is not concerned with the revelation of God. The one exalts or, at least, emphasizes what man has done; the other honours God as the One who has graciously given to sinful man a word of redemption. How good God has been to give such a word! How wondrous are His ways and His thoughts past finding out. May God grant to us all the sincere desire and the will earnestly to follow the example of Him who, "beginning at Moses and all the prophets, he expounded unto them in all the scriptures the things concerning himself". (Luke xxiv, 27)

NOTES TO LECTURE IV

1. Geerhardus Vos: *The Self-Disclosure of Jesus*, New York, 1926, pp. 11–34.
2. *Op. cit.*, p. 19.
3. *Op. cit.*, p. 24.
4. Cf. Vos's discussion of this term, *op. cit.*, pp. 235 ff.
5. The noun is of the *qaṭṭāl* form.
6. *'ēl* probably stands as an appositional genitive before *gibbôr*. Cf. G. A. Smith: *The Book of Isaiah*, Vol. I, New York, 1927, p. 135.
7. E.g. Daniel, vii.
8. Cf. Charles Hodge: *Systematic Theology*, London, 1872, Vol. II, p. 388.
9. *Op. cit.*, p. 389.
10. Karl Barth: *Kirchliche Dogmatik* IV: 2. pp. 6, 37, 117.
11. *Op. cit.*, p. 390.
12. *Op. cit.*, IV: 2, p. 37—"sie ist mit seiner Gottheit Zusammen integrierendes Moment des Christusgeschehens".
13. *Op. cit.*, IV: 2, p. 92.

14. For an excellent study of the philosophical background of the theology of crisis, cf. Cornelius Van Til: *The New Modernism*, Philadelphia, 1946.
15. This is the literal force of the Hebrew.